The World Aflame

Dan Jones
&
Marina Amaral

with Mark Hawkins-Dady

The World Aflame

THE LONG WAR
1914 TO 1945

HEAD
of ZEUS

An Apollo Book

An Apollo book
First published in the UK in 2020 by Head of Zeus Ltd
This paperback first published in the UK in 2021 by
Head of Zeus Ltd

9 7 5 3 1 2 4 6 8

A CIP catalogue record for this book is available from the
British Library.

ISBN [PB] 9781789544664
ISBN [E] 9781789542028

Design by Isambard Thomas / CORVO
Typesetting by Adrian McLaughlin
Colour reproduction by DawkinsColour
Printed in Serbia by Publikum d.o.o

Head of Zeus Ltd
5–8 Hardwick Street, London ECIR 4RG
WWW.HEADOFZEUS.COM

Previous page
French soldiers in a trench on the Western Front, during
the First World War

Overleaf
Children in Kent take cover during the Battle of Britain,
summer 1940

PICTURE CREDITS

All images © Getty Images,
except

p.102: Siege of Kut © Alamy;
pp.148–9 POWs © US
National Archives;
pp.172–3 Anna Coleman Ladd
© Library of Congress;
pp.338–9 Czeslawa Kwoka
© Auschwitz Memorial and
Museum

ACKNOWLEDGMENTS

The authors would like to
thank Anthony and Nic
Cheetham, Richard Milbank,
Clémence Jacquinet, Matilda
Singer, Dan Groenewald and
all the team at Head of Zeus.
Thank you also to Paul Reed.

Introduction

On 28 July 1946, in the north-eastern French region called Meuse, the general and statesman Charles de Gaulle reflected on the troubled history of his times. A generation previously, men had dug deep, muddy, miserable trenches through the ground thereabouts, and monstrous armies equipped with hellish new weapons had fought a battle nearly a year in duration. Then, in 1944, troops had once again torn through the same, barely recovered countryside, bludgeoning out the endgame of another appalling conflict, slaughtering each other and innocent civilians.

De Gaulle spoke of these things with grim, heroic reverence: they were 'the greatest events in our history', requiring those who suffered through them 'to guard intact the force of their souls'. More than that, he argued, the events amounted to a tragic 'war of thirty years'. In other words, they were flare-ups in a single great conflagration, which had raged during the first half of the twentieth century. Just as seventeenth-century Europe had endured one Thirty Years War, suggested de Gaulle, so the modern world had suffered another – an idea toyed with also by Britain's wartime prime minister, Winston Churchill, in his historical memoirs. Today, historians are much more comfortable in thinking about the First World War of 1914–18 and the Second World War of 1939–45 as close but separate conflicts. But whatever the terminology, most people would agree with

Churchill's judgement that the events of 1914–45 amounted to 'the two supreme cataclysms of recorded history'.

This book is a journey through those wartime years. It is a history in colour. It contains 200 photographs, all of which were originally shot in black and white, and each of which has been colourized here. Each picture is paired with explanatory text to give historical context, and the book proceeds in more or less chronological sequence, so that it can be studied piecemeal or read from cover to cover. It is not an attempt to impose (or reimpose) a grand new historical shape on the events it describes. Rather, it is a book that asks you to look at a story that has been told many times over, but in a new light.

Colourizing historical photos is not an exact science. It is a delicate and technical process that requires, on the one hand, diligent historical research and, on the other, the use of what can be called – without apology – artistic licence. Colourization does not – cannot – 'restore' anything, for there are no hidden colours to hunt for. Instead, it adds them, based on known facts and responsible guesswork. It is an interpretive tool, whose limitations must never be brushed over or forgotten.

This does not mean that colourization is frivolous or 'fake'. It is self-evident that we respond to colour instinctively, in ways that stir our hearts as well as our heads. Colourization at its best is an emotional enhancing agent: it magnifies empathy and horror, pity and disgust. It challenges us to respond to history not simply as accountants and analysts, but as feeling beings, capable of the same fear, confusion, passion, ambition, anger and love as those whose images we see. It asks us to ask more. It nudges us to go off and hunt for the truth behind these extraordinary scenes. That is its purpose and its power.

Assembling 200 photographs that do justice to the history of the First and Second World Wars (and conflicts in between) was a hard and sometimes harrowing process. We hope this selection tells a story that honours the times it narrates, while knowing that it can only ever be partial. Miles of books have been written on the topics we mention; in many cases, a single photograph and its context have spawned an entire scholarship. We offer in advance our apologies for any omissions and errors, all of which are our own. But we hope that this book will inspire readers new to the topic to delve deeper into the history, and encourage older heads to reconsider what they think they know.

While working on this book, we passed the centenary of the end of the First World War, and the eightieth anniversary of the start of the Second World War. We heard all too often of the deaths of veterans of the latter conflict. In relatively few years, the last of that wartime generation will be lost to the world, and their deeds and experiences will become solely the preserve of history, and not living memory. We offer this book in part as a tribute to those men and women – some of them heroes, some of them victims, and others just ordinary people who lived through terrifying times.

We also offer this book as a warning. Fascism, nationalism, populism, anti-Semitism, hatred, bigotry, racism and the politics of exclusion, division and isolation have been on the march once more all over the world – a world that is fragile. It takes less than we think to set it aflame.

Marina Amaral *&* Dan Jones
Belo Horizonte *and* Staines-upon-Thames

End of an Era

On 20 May 1910, London glittered. Nine kings and emperors, augmented by myriad princes, princesses and potentates, gathered to mourn a man styled 'By the Grace of God, of the United Kingdom of Great Britain and Ireland and the British Dominions beyond the Seas, King, Defender of the Faith, Emperor of India'. King Edward VII was being buried.

First among equals at the ceremonies was Edward's only surviving son and successor, King George V (pictured centre). He would pick up where his grandparents Victoria and Albert had left off, resetting the constitutional monarchy along the lines of probity and duty. By George's side, pride of place as a chief mourner went to his first cousin, the prickly, complex and impetuous Kaiser Wilhelm II of Germany. He can be seen here, gripping the reins of his horse with his 'withered' arm, the legacy of a difficult birth, as the procession neared London's

Paddington Station to continue on to Windsor. In London, Wilhelm found himself in the heart of an empire he envied, whose navy outclassed his own, and whose new-found bonhomie with France seemed (to him) to be aimed at boxing in Germany.

The king these mourners came to bury had exceeded expectations. During his long tenure as Prince of Wales and heir to the throne, he had indulged his appetites so freely that his mother, Victoria, had despaired. Yet in his brief reign, which began in 1901, Edward had played to his strengths: charm, an international outlook and some adroit diplomacy. His personal efforts had helped to secure the Anglo-French agreement of 1904 known as the Entente Cordiale, which replaced years of friction.

In the backward-shining light that history throws, the Edwardian Age (extended by historians to the summer of 1914) is often presented as a time of optimism, promise and the casting off of Victorian primness. Yet it was also a time of turbulence in a not-so-United Kingdom. Trade unionists flexed their muscles. The Labour Party made electoral advances. Women demanded the vote, some militantly. And the question of Home Rule in Ireland threatened to explode, as Irish nationalist and loyalist paramilitaries began arming themselves. Edwardian Britain also had to engage with a continental Europe that had slipped into confrontational blocs. Since the Battle of Waterloo in 1815, Britain had pursued imperial and economic expansion while avoiding European entanglements. Now, things were changing.

Most palpable among the new European realities was the fact of a united, Prussian-dominated Germany at Europe's heart, bitterly opposed by a France still all too aware of the prestige and territory lost during the Franco-Prussian War of 1870–71. By 1910, Germany's industrial output pipped Britain's and far exceeded

France's. Yet German democratic institutions remained relatively weak – which meant that the Kaiser and his militarymen still wielded disproportionate power. Wilhelm II had abandoned the strategic caution of his grandfather Wilhelm I, dispensed with the services of the elderly master-statesman Otto von Bismarck, and allowed a carefully calibrated relationship with Russia to lapse in favour of consolidating relations with Austria-Hungary. That spurred France and Russia into making their own entente, effectively a mutual defence pact, which Germany interpreted as a threatening encirclement. Britain's Entente Cordiale with France fell short of this sort of defensive alliance. Nevertheless, Germany could see that Britain had chosen sides in the great geopolitical game.

As alliances shifted among the Western powers, further east lay the 'sick man of Europe': the Ottoman Empire. As it was steadily dispossessed of its European provinces, the retreating empire spat out newly independent nations – and new risks for the international system. 'The Balkans' became a byword for instability. None of this should suggest that the rest of the world was a haven of calm. Bloody revolutions gripped Mexico and China in 1910 and 1911 respectively. Still, the most immediate dangers plainly lay in Europe, where the system of formal alliances held the possibility for catastrophe. Against that background, as almost the entire monarchy of Europe gathered in London to pay their respects to Edward VII, they were unwittingly marking the end of an era. Within less than a decade, many of these kings would have no thrones to occupy. For millions of their subjects, an even worse fate was in store.

The Belle Epoque

As Edward VII discovered during his apprenticeship as Prince of Wales, Paris was Europe's playground, full of the louche delights of the 'Belle Époque' – the near half-century of relative stability before 1914, when the arts, progressive thought and good living flourished in Europe's leading cities. No corner of Paris exemplified *joie de vivre* as well as the Moulin Rouge in Montmartre – known for the high-kicking, flesh-and-bloomers-revealing can-can. Depicted here is the Moulin's rear 'garden', with dancers and tutus, assorted clientele – and an extraordinary hollow elephant; its recreational uses were said to have included a hideaway for opium-smoking.

There was, however, a darker side to these years of gaiety and pleasure, and fractures and insecurities in French society were beginning to be exposed. France had been humiliated by the Prussian Army in 1871, when a newly unified German Empire was proclaimed on French soil, at Versailles. With wings clipped, territory lost, a declining population – and now a large, industrially vibrant and militarily dynamic German power as a neighbour – the French, and especially their politicians and military chiefs, had plenty to worry about.

New Americans

A world away from Old Europe and its global empires lay the optimistic and energetic United States. Many of the new Americans fanning out towards the Pacific Ocean were poorer European migrants, tempted by the promise of land, absence of persecution and the opportunity to make (or remake) themselves in a land where continental expansion, at the expense of native peoples, had been piously called 'Manifest Destiny'. In the 1910 census, nearly 12 million Americans reported having been born in Europe; this photograph captures one small, wide-eyed group of recent arrivals, enjoying a first Christmas dinner in their adopted home.

Although the USA traditionally avoided Old World conflicts, its increasing power and demographic change meant that it could not remain aloof forever. By 1910, US industrial production was equivalent to that of Britain, Germany and France put together. This bald statistic, combined with the generations-old and constantly refreshed ties between the Old and New Worlds, meant that when Europe descended into war, the USA's manifest destiny proved in fact to lie on battlefields across the Atlantic.

The Machine Age

In a rapidly industrializing world, few inventions symbolized the new, mechanized era better than the Ford Model T – not merely a car, but a phenomenon, which confirmed that the era of the automobile had truly arrived. The Model T was not at all glamorous, but it became an icon of modernity in a country that was perfectly primed for motor cars – with virgin land being everywhere transformed into neat, gridlined suburbs.

Henry Ford's genius as an industrialist lay less in pure innovation – the motor car was invented in Europe after all – but in adaptation and clever production techniques, which drove down costs from an initial $825 per vehicle in 1908 to $290 by 1927. Mechanization of the sort that Ford embraced changed the lives of travellers, workers, businesspeople and consumers. Yet its contribution to human ease and economic efficiency soon had to be weighed against something much grimmer: a global conflict defined by the mass production of weapons and the spectre of mechanized killing.

The Era of Flight

While Henry Ford accelerated the motor car era, other entrepreneurs were looking to the skies. In 1903, American brothers Orville and Wilbur Wright made the first major machine-powered flight. Aircraft manufacture soon proliferated in Europe and the United States, and in 1909 Glenn Curtiss's Manufacturing Company launched the Curtiss 'pusher', a classic design. In these fragile assemblages of metal, canvas, rope and wood – like a tricycle with wings – the pilot sat exposed, pushed along by the propeller to his rear.

Military minds soon began co-opting the technology of powered flight. In this photograph (1912), Thomas DeWitt Milling tests out a Curtiss pusher for the US Army at College Park, Maryland; by this time, Curtiss pushers had already made their first take-offs and landings on naval vessels. Far away, meanwhile, over the deserts of Libya, Italian airmen conducted the first operations in which bombs were dropped from an aircraft. By 1917, Milling was supervising the training of US Army pilots for Europe's war zone. Air power's age of innocence had lasted little more than a decade.

A Naval Arms Race

The invention of aeroplanes suggested that Britain's traditional line of defence against invasion – the sea – might not be the bulwark it once was. All the same, few doubted that the British Empire's security still rested fundamentally on the Royal Navy, whose global pre-eminence seemed to be confirmed by the launch, in 1906, of HMS *Dreadnought*, pictured here. The most advanced warship in the world, she was powered by turbine engines, boasted a fearsome array of guns with advanced targeting capabilities, and could speed through the seas at up to 21 knots.

Kaiser Wilhelm II took envious note and tasked his naval chief with expanding the strength of the German navy, the Kaiserliche Marine, launching an Anglo-German arms race. Between 1906 and 1912, both nations threw money and resources into shipbuilding, and soon even *Dreadnought*'s design was outclassed by successors. This competition proved to be a popular patriotic effort, and despite British anxieties, the Royal Navy retained its superiority. After accepting that they could not outmuscle the British in shipbuilding, German strategists began looking to a different sort of vessel to make up the difference: submarines.

Mexico at War

In the years before 1914, the British Empire remained the most extensive empire in the world. By contrast, Spain's had shrunk to virtually nothing. Mexico had long ago wrenched itself free (1823). However, independence had done little to create an enduring political settlement and in 1910 this boiled over into revolution, as Mexico's long-standing autocrat Porfirio Díaz tried to cling on to power. For years Díaz had modernized and enriched the country but at the cost of extreme inequality and rampant corruption.

A key figure in the many-stranded conflict that comprised the Mexican Revolution and civil war was the colourful, radical figure of Emiliano Zapata Salazar (*front row, fifth from left, in dark jacket*), whose calls for land redistribution spawned a manifesto (*Plan de Ayala*) and an eponymous movement ('Zapatismo'). The Zapatistas helped topple Díaz in 1911, only to find themselves embroiled in many subsequent years of civil war. Zapata's life would end violently in a 1919, but his legend lived on.

Young Winston

As First Lord of the Admiralty from 1911, Winston Churchill was in his element, propelling the British naval expansion to contain the German threat. Here, clear-eyed and fresh-faced, the young Winston exudes the self-confidence that became both his greatest strength and, sometimes, his siren weakness.

By his thirties, Churchill had already trained as a cavalry officer, worked as a war reporter in South Africa, escaped from a Boer prison camp, become a Conservative MP (1900), crossed the floor to join the Liberal Party (1904) – thereby enraging his former colleagues – and then, in government, pursued social reform as President of the Board of Trade. A tenure as Home Secretary followed (1910–11), during which he struggled with tensions in Ireland and the perplexing challenge (to much of the male political class) of the campaign for women's suffrage, which was taking a militant turn.

For many a politician and statesman, Churchill's career to date would have already represented a life's work. In fact, he had barely begun.

The End of Imperial China

While Mexico was consumed by conflict, across the Pacific Ocean violent uprisings reverberated through China in 1911. They produced these beheadings, by which the authorities intimidated potential rebels. China had no long-in-the-tooth strongman to overthrow, but rather an enfeebled court government and a child-emperor, Puyi – the eleventh ruler of the Qing dynasty and, as it transpired, the last.

On 10 October 1911, troops mutinied in the Wuchang insurrection, which in turn sparked the Xinhai uprising, under the leadership of veteran revolutionary Sun Yat-sen. On 12 February 1912, Puyi abdicated, and two millennia of Chinese imperial rule ended. In their place came a provisional government, under the experienced politician Yuan Shikai.

But the future held more turbulence. Sun founded the profoundly influential Guomindang (or Kuomintang) political movement, while thousands of Chinese would contribute to the coming world war, mainly as labourers for the French.

The Balkan Tinderbox

The dissolution of another age-old empire, the Ottoman, had begun in the nineteenth century. In the Balkans it left behind uncertain borders, vying nationalist interests and fragile new states. In October 1912, Serbia, Bulgaria, Greece and Montenegro formed a 'Balkan League' against Ottoman Turkey, during which time this photograph – showing League troops on the Serbian–Bulgarian border – was taken.

The First Balkan War was a short, sharp affair, over within two months. It pushed back the Ottoman Empire's European border all the way to Constantinople (Istanbul) and eastern Thrace, while Albania achieved independence, and the League allies carved up the province of Macedonia among themselves. But in 1913, Bulgaria, unhappy with its share of the spoils, attacked its erstwhile allies and began the Second Balkan War.

The Balkans were often described as a 'tinderbox', and the events of 1912–13 seemed to bear out the cliché. Just as worrying, these Balkan wars presented a dangerous illusion: that modern wars could be managed to deliver quick results. The hazards of such thinking soon became apparent.

Descent to War

Everything changed in Europe on 28 June 1914. That morning, a pro-Serbian assassin named Gavrilo Princip killed Archduke Franz Ferdinand, heir to the Austro-Hungarian imperial throne. A few weeks later, all across Europe, millions of people were mobilizing for war; Franz Ferdinand's death had sent the continent spiralling towards a major conflict. Duty called, and young men were bidding what they hoped would be a temporary farewell to sweethearts, families and friends.

As troops signed up and moved out, there was plenty of bravado. Ernst Jünger, twentieth-century Germany's most famous war diarist, recalled departing 'in a rain of flowers, in a drunken atmosphere of blood and roses. Surely the war had to supply us with what we wanted; the great, the overwhelming, the hallowed experience... Anything to participate, not to have to stay at home!' Yet for all this triumphalism – which was by no means confined to Germany – every individual parting would also have embraced the quieter emotions: fear, nervous excitement, anxiety, uncertainty. Would they come home? And if so, when?

For a while during July, the leaders of Europe's great powers had a chance to escape the conflagration many of them had long feared. Instead, the complex and delicate networks of allegiance that bound together Europe's most populous and powerful nations (and their empires) had all been activated at once. In place of containment came escalation.

The process by which the shooting of the archduke became a world war was both simple and dizzyingly complex. In the end, it boiled down to a few stark events. Diplomacy failed, and on 28 July Austria-Hungary declared war on Serbia, confident of German backing. In response, Russia vowed to defend Serbia, a position that France was treaty-bound to support. On 1 August, Germany therefore declared war on Russia, and, two days later, on France as well. By 4 August, Britain and her empire, including Canada, Australia, New Zealand and South Africa, had entered the fray, and the foreign secretary, Sir Edward Grey, had unforgettably remarked: 'The lamps are going out all over Europe; we shall not see them lit again in our lifetime.'

Yet at least as well known as Grey's elegiac prediction was its precise opposite: the jaunty and glib forecast that the war would 'all be over by Christmas'. Such confidence relied on war being as easy to end as it was to begin. As the lamps went out, they were replaced by the roar of engines, the smoking stacks of steam trains, and the hiss of ship's turbines to speed men and machines to where they needed to be. Germany's war plan was almost a railway timetable in itself: all aboard for Belgium, and onward into France for, it was hoped, a quick victory. The Belgians put up a struggle before, inevitably, being knocked down, their forts bombed into piles of concrete.

As Germans poured into Belgium and France, Russians poured – surprisingly quickly – into Germany, as did the French. A British Expeditionary Force landed in France, not to invade but to help, but it was painfully small in number. Austro-Hungarian armies penetrated Serbia three times, but Serbia stood firm, for the time being. Invasions were not limited to Europe, for this was a conflict of empires. Germany's colonies across Africa came under attack, especially where there were important communications sites to neutralize. Much further east, Japan piled in as well, beginning to realize her own imperial dreams, while in British India volunteer soldiers headed up the gangplanks onto ships, bound for unknown destinations.

Within weeks, the declarations of war had led to death and destruction on an industrial scale. By the start of the winter of 1914–15, the list of casualties – dead, wounded, missing or captured – on all sides had already reached two million. Historic city centres such as Louvain, as well as scores of rural towns and villages across north-eastern France and Belgium, lay in ruins.

So the war was not over by Christmas. But by December 1914, it was over for hundreds of thousands of young servicemen who had taken their leave of loved ones less than five months previously. For them, the promise of reunion contained in *auf Wiedersehen* had been overtaken by the finality of 'goodbye'.

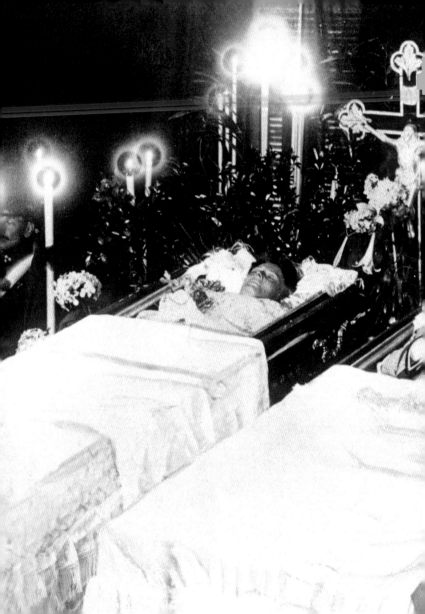

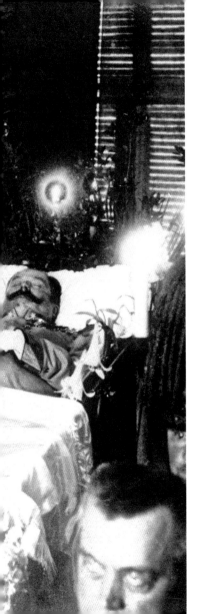

Franz Ferdinand

On 28 June 1914, Archduke Franz Ferdinand – heir presumptive to the imperial throne of Austria-Hungary – was accompanied by his wife, Sophie Chotek, in a motorcade through Sarajevo, capital of the troubled province of Bosnia-Herzegovina.

As the couple were driven through the city, they were attacked by assassins associated with the secret military society known as the 'Black Hand'. Despite this, the archduke continued on his way to Sarajevo's town hall for speeches. After leaving, his car took a wrong turning and was forced to stop momentarily outside a café where one of the would-be assassins, Gavrilo Princip, was able to fire off his pistol at close range. The couple were fatally wounded. This photograph shows them lying in repose before their funeral.

Their deaths were much more than a personal tragedy. Austria-Hungary – supported by Germany – immediately blamed and threatened Serbia; Russia, allied with France, took the opposing side. Neither would back down, and Europe's spiral to war began. The archduke's murder proved enough not only to light the Balkan tinderbox, but to set the continent ablaze.

The Tsar Declares War

In the summer of 1914, first cousins Tsar Nicholas II and Kaiser Wilhelm II exchanged telegrams, each pleading with the other to avert a catastrophe. It came to nothing. Germany declared war on Russia on 1 August.

On 2 August the Tsar attended a religious service at the Winter Palace in St Petersburg, his capital – very soon to be renamed Petrograd. Later, he strode onto the palace balcony to read out Russia's reciprocal declaration of war. When this photograph was taken, thousands of his subjects were thronging the vast space of the square below him, some waving Russian tricolour flags. They cheered as Nicholas spoke of Slav brotherhood in the face of Austrian aggression and attacked Germany's failure to understand that Russian mobilization was merely a defensive measure.

Now, he said, the time had come to uphold Russia's status and honour. Russians should cast aside their differences, reaffirm their bond with their Tsar and prepare for self-sacrifice. The coming clash of arms would test Russians' enthusiasm for conflict – and royal rule – to breaking point.

To War, By Train

Germany declared war on France on 3 August 1914. Later the same day, France made its own declaration of war. Although France lagged behind Germany in wealth, population, technology and resources, she had a well-developed rail network that was now pressed into action, transporting nearly two million men to defend the borders.

The reservists of the 6th Territorial Infantry Regiment, pictured here boarding at Dunkirk in August 1914, are wearing the blue greatcoats, red kepis and red trousers that symbolized French military pride. A desire to blend into the environment had influenced the dress of the German, British and Russian armies, but such utilitarian drabness was unacceptable to the French. In particular, the bright red trousers, the *pantalon rouge*, were totemic. They denoted French fearlessness, which informed a strand of French military belief in *l'attaque à outrance* – relentless offensive action. To tinker with that tradition, the thinking went, could undermine the French fighting spirit.

The Schlieffen Plan

German mobilization in the west demanded its own colossal rail effort. At the outbreak of war, troops commenced what would be more than 40,000 train journeys from Cologne's Hauptbahnhof, from where they were transported across Europe. Moving manpower on this epic scale was no mean feat, but it was essential to fulfil the strategic aims of the so-called Schlieffen Plan, named after the late German chief-of-staff, Alfred von Schlieffen (1833–1913).

Formulated in the 1890s, the strategy suggested that the best way to win against a Franco-Russian alliance would be a six-week attack on France in the west before tackling Russia in the east. To that end, invasion forces should be routed through Luxembourg and neutral Belgium, bypassing fortified French borders. Belgium's modest army was no match and by 17 August 1914 Brussels was abandoned as German troops poured into the country. The invading forces pictured here, in the aftermath of Belgium's capitulation, are enjoying a meal from a field kitchen. German troops would continue to occupy Belgian cities for four years.

Fear and Flight

As German troops invaded and the Belgian Army was thrown into a fighting retreat, thousands of ordinary Belgians were also on the move, fleeing to safety. Those pictured here were lucky enough to have motor transport to take them to the cobbled streets of Paris; others were forced to trudge for miles along roads and fields.

As they retreated, Belgians enraged their attackers by destroying bridges and railway lines, slowing the Schlieffen Plan. In response, German military chiefs chose to regard a whole raft of defensive Belgian actions as illegal warfare – or terrorism. Within days of the invasion of Belgium, reports began to circulate of an uncompromising German policy of mass punishment executions and the razing of whole villages.

Events in Belgium shocked the world and turned minds against Germany, including in the United States. German brutality brought about the deaths of some 6,000 Belgians under occupation; but it was also a powerful propaganda tool for the Allies, whose recruitment messages for the rest of the war would be morally as well as patriotically charged.

Prince Edward and the BEF

Many Germans hoped that Britain would keep out of the war, but the Entente Cordiale with France was taken seriously, as was Britain's long-standing treaty commitment to guarantee Belgian neutrality. Britain declared war on 4 August 1914. A week later, one eager new lieutenant began his officer training. In this photograph, the twenty-year-old Edward, Prince of Wales, parades in London, dwarfed by the older and more seasoned men of the 1st Battalion Grenadier Guards, to which he was attached.

New recruits were indeed in great demand; the British Expeditionary Force (BEF) crossing the Channel on 7 August numbered only 100,000 men. But already, civilians were flocking in their thousands to the recruiting stations, answering War Secretary Lord Kitchener's exhortations for 'New Armies'. Kitchener also approved Prince Edward's pleas to be allowed over to France. King George's anxieties meant Edward was kept out of firefights; but, seconded to BEF headquarters, he threw himself into his duties and earned the respect of those under his command.

Aggression in Africa

In 1885, during the 'Scramble for Africa', European statesmen had tried to ensure that their colonies on the African continent could claim neutrality in any future European conflict. Within days of the outbreak of war, those hopes had been roundly squashed. In fact, the very first 'British' rifle shot of the entire war is credited to an African recruit of the Gold Coast Regiment, some of whose members are shown here, during rifle inspection.

Germany's colonies in Africa were weak and exposed, bordered by the numerous colonies of their enemies. So it was that two weeks before any soldier of the BEF fired at the enemy in Belgium, the Allies had captured their first capital – in West Africa. From the British colony of Gold Coast (now Ghana) and then from French West Africa, small forces converged on German Togoland (now Togo), reaching the city of Lomé on 7/8 August. On 26 August, Togoland unconditionally surrendered. First blood had been drawn in a theatre of war that would expand rapidly, bringing fighting across the length and breadth of the African continent for the next four years.

The Battle of Tannenberg

While the BEF and the French Army fell back before the German advance through western Europe, the citizens of East Prussia, at Germany's north-eastern edge, were reeling in the face of a terrifying shock. Germany's military chiefs had comforted themselves that Russia's conscript army, though massive, was badly led and poorly equipped, so would spend weeks preparing itself for war. They were therefore deeply alarmed when, in mid-August 1914, two Russian armies marched into East Prussia, sending the German Eighth Army into retreat and threatening the East Prussian capital at Königsberg. A replacement general, Paul von Hindenburg, was scrambled into place to defend the Second Reich.

This photograph shows Russian prisoners being transported by rail in the aftermath of an engagement that became known as the Battle of Tannenberg – in reference to a medieval conflict fought in similar territory in the year 1410. Tannenberg was a German triumph, a Russian disaster, and made Hindenburg Germany's darling.

The Miracle of the Marne

While Russian armies were being mauled at Tannenberg, in France Marshal Joseph Joffre, the French chief-of-staff, was demanding assistance from the battered BEF for a grand if desperate counter-attack, along the River Marne. The threat to France was rapidly becoming existential. To that end, Joffre sacked commanders, reconfigured his armies, and used every mode of transport to rush men and machines into position to resist.

From 5 September, the Allies attacked German positions between Paris and the fortress city of Verdun. The assault was dubbed a 'miracle', since it forced the Germans back to fixed defences along the River Aisne. But this photograph makes plain the terrible price that was paid. Here, in the normally quiet commune of Maurupt-le-Montois, lay lines of shattered bodies. They added to the carpets of death already visible across north-eastern France. German casualties were mounting, but for ordinary French servicemen – the *poilus* – no phase of the war was as deadly as its first weeks.

The Seventy-Five

The 'Miracle of the Marne' in September 1914 saved Paris, averted an Allied catastrophe and left Germany's Schlieffen Plan in tatters. An essential component of the victory – and of later battles – was the 75mm field gun, seen here during French Army exercises in 1909. First developed in 1897, it was a revolutionary weapon with a sophisticated mechanism and a more rapid rate of fire than anything invented before it. Other armies adopted their own versions of the 75mm. The British had the 18-pounder, the Germans a 77mm gun. But the *soixante-quinze*, as it was known, bested them all.

However, while the French had the best type of light gun, they lacked the diversity of artillery of their enemies. True, the French defenders didn't need monster howitzers, pulled by thirty-six horses, of the kind with which Germany had pulverized the forts of Belgium during the early days of the war. But the struggle in the west was about to develop in a way that would call for many, many more – and larger – guns.

Nursing the Wounded

Although wounded soldiers had previously been left on the battlefield to fend for themselves, by the early twentieth century care for those injured in combat was part of the basic expectations of warfare. And the appallingly bloody first weeks of the war in 1914 confirmed the need for medical operations of unprecedented proportions.

Military nursing care had made great strides since the days of Florence Nightingale in the Crimean War of the 1850s and it provided a way for women to contribute directly to the war effort. Women's voluntary organizations sprang up across the warring nations, generally staffed by discreet, unattached young women of respectable backgrounds, who did not need to earn a living.

Less respectable, certainly less discreet, but much more famous than most of these volunteers was the avant-garde Russian-born dancer Ida Rubinstein, pictured here. In taking up nursing duties in Paris, she swapped the exotic and risqué costumes of her stage roles for a nurse's 'uniform' – in her case, a striking flowing garment designed by artist Léon Bakst.

Ypres and the Indian Army

In the autumn of 1914, as the British Expeditionary Force fought tooth and nail, around Ypres, to prevent German seizure of the vital Channel ports, they needed nurses as much as any army. Since August, the ranks of the regular BEF had been shredded. So, into Europe there now arrived contingents of the largest volunteer army in the world: the Indian Army. Landing at Marseilles in late September, Indian divisions reached the theatre of conflict by travelling the entire length of France overland – on foot, on horseback, by train and in fleets of requisitioned London buses.

From 22 October, they joined battle. Immediately, members of the Indian Army were dying and nursing wounds, like this group being visited by King George V. Marking the arrival of Indian troops on the Western Front, the king had sent an official welcome: 'I look to all my Indian soldiers to uphold the British Raj against an aggressive and relentless enemy.' During the course of the war, eleven Indian soldiers would be awarded the Victoria Cross.

The Masurian Lakes

On the Eastern Front, Germany's triumph at the Battle of Tannenberg had smashed the Russian Second Army. However, the Russian First Army remained on East Prussian soil. To deal with this threat, General Hindenburg and his chief-of-staff, Erich Ludendorff, gathered their forces to move against the Russians around the waterways and forests known collectively as the Masurian Lakes. The Russians were forced to retreat towards the border, suffering another 100,000 dead, wounded and captured. Although the East Prussian adventure was not the end of Russian designs on Germany, the echo of these heavy defeats rang in Russian ears for a long time.

In this photograph, German machine-gunners are manning a position near the East Prussian town of Darkehmen (now Ozyorsk, Russia). Infantrymen on all sides in this war feared their vulnerability in an attack against heavy machine-gun positions. In raw statistics, machine guns did not kill as many men as did artillery, but machine guns instilled their own form of terror as the scythe of the battlefield, often aimed low to cut men down at the knees.

The Christmas Truce

On the Western Front, nothing was quick. The First Battle of Ypres continued into mid-November, when a miserable Flanders winter set in. The fallacy of the idea that the war would be won in months was sinking in. Yet before the era of trench warfare truly began, a wholly unexpected interlude reminded combatants of their shared humanity. In stretches of the British and French sectors, for a few short hours the firing stopped for Christmas.

With their hands raised just in case, soldiers from both sides ventured into no-man's land, communicating by gesture, by drinking together, by singing and in some places by impromptu games of football. They swapped presents including items of uniform, as seen here among this mingled group from the 104th and 106th Saxon regiments and the London Rifle Brigade at Ploegsteert in Belgium. Senior commanders hated it. Had the war truly been 'over by Christmas' as the optimists had proclaimed, it would have been a beautiful ending.

A Widening War

n late 1915, the British writer William Thomson Hill published a slim volume entitled *The Martyrdom of Nurse Cavell*. Its subtitle was equally forthright: *The Life Story of the Victim of Germany's Most Barbarous Crime*. This was a bold claim, to say the least. After everything that 1915 had thrown up, there was no lack of competition for the title of Most Atrocious Deed committed in the name of the Kaiser. Yet somehow, amid all this, a vicar's daughter from Norfolk achieved a form of secular sainthood, her life and fate coming to epitomize what the British, in particular, told themselves they were fighting for.

Born in Swardeston, near Norwich, in December 1865, Edith Cavell enjoyed a happy childhood. After boarding school, she worked as a governess in Essex and later in Belgium before, in 1896, gravitating towards nursing. Cavell trained for two years in London and rose in the profession's ranks. This photograph shows her in 1903, when she was assistant matron at Shoreditch

Infirmary (now St Leonard's Hospital, Hackney). Although visiting her mother in Norfolk in summer 1914, she travelled back to Belgium on the outbreak of war, for she felt duty called – and by this time she was matron in charge of a landmark training school for new nurses, the École Belge d'Infirmières Diplômées in Brussels.

The rapid German advance meant that by 20 August Brussels was already behind the lines. Cavell's nursing school now also became a discreet refuge for Allied soldiers and Belgians evading the occupation authorities – part of a covert network that provided them with hiding places, false documentation and a route over the Belgian border to safety in the neutral Netherlands.

It was a risky enterprise, and eventually, on 8 August 1915, Cavell was arrested. In prison for ten weeks, she refused to lie about her activities and signed a statement that served as an admission of guilt. While she was in solitary confinement, the US and Spanish ministers to Belgium attempted to intercede on her behalf, but to no avail. Cavell was court-martialled and sentenced to death for 'war treason'. Within forty-eight hours, early on 12 October 1915, she donned her matron's uniform one last time to face the firing squad. Her reputed final words, as carved into her post-war London monument, were: 'Patriotism is not enough. I must have no hatred or bitterness for anyone.'

Uproar followed. Britain's foreign secretary, Sir Edward Grey, felt her death would be received 'with horror and disgust not only in the Allied States but throughout the civilized world'. Cavell's execution was immediately exploited by the British propaganda machine to incite hatred and bitterness towards the Germans. It was not hard to do, for the execution cemented a growing international impression of Hunnish barbarism already fuelled by the sinking of the passenger liners RMS *Lusitania* (off Ireland) and SS *Arabic*, and the bombing of civilians from airships.

On the battlefields themselves, the trenches begun in 1914 continued to expand and fast came to define the Western Front. As soldiers adapted to subterranean lives worsened by boredom, squalor, noise and danger, their commanders puzzled over how to break the deadlock. Ever more artillery seemed the answer, but, as the British found, their factories struggled to produce enough shells. Thousands of new women workers, the 'munitionettes', came to the rescue as the government invested in arms manufacturing. And when the Germans unleashed poison gas at Ypres, soon all sides were experimenting with this new and loathsome battlefield weapon.

The boundaries of war spread, too. In 1915, Italy threw in her lot with the Allies and rushed to attack Austria, beginning an icy mountain war. Meanwhile, further east, Austrians tried to forestall an invasion by Russia. In November 1914, the Ottoman Empire joined the Central Powers, and between February and October 1915 fended off an Allied assault on the Gallipoli peninsula, despite heroic efforts by troops from Australia and New Zealand. But elsewhere, Ottoman defeat by the Russians in the Caucasus mountains led to a genocidal massacre of ethnic Armenians, who were made scapegoats for Ottoman defeat.

As the First World War widened and deepened in 1915, so the mood of the world darkened. The selfless courageous of those like Edith Cavell provided rare but beautiful points of light.

U-boats

Britain's position as a world superpower owed much to the Royal Navy. But British ships were not invincible, and the hazard naval commanders feared the most were the Kaiser's submarines, or U-boats (from *Unterseeboot*, literally 'undersea boat'). Experiments with building U-boats had taken place in Germany since the 1850s, and manufacturing them had become a key element of Kaiser Wilhelm II's pre-war naval strategy.

Fighting aboard U-boats was arduous. Sailors had to deal with the cramped, hot, dangerous and claustrophobic nature of life below the waves, as this image of submariners doing checks in a U-boat's oil-powered engine room suggests. But submarines were potent weapons of war. Between 1914 and 1918, around 2,600 vessels were sunk by underwater attacks. Germany's most successful U-boat commander of the war, Lothar von Arnauld de la Perière, was single-handedly responsible for destroying nearly half a million tons of shipping. Numbers like these represented a menace pitched perfectly to excite the fears of an island nation.

69

War in Mesopotamis

As war spread below the seas, so it entered new lands, including those of the Ottoman Empire, whose territory still extended from Constantinople across Anatolia and into the Arabian Peninsula, and whose sultan claimed spiritual supremacy over the Sunni Muslim world. Yet Ottoman Turkey was an empire in search of friends. Historically hostile to Russia, by 1914 Turkey was also chilly towards Britain. Yet at the same time, the Ottomans had forged closer links with Germany, based on a mutual interest in the (incomplete) Berlin–Baghdad railway, a section of which is shown in this photograph.

Although the Ottoman government pretended neutrality at the outbreak of war, in August 1914 members of the pro-war 'Young Turk' faction, including the minister for war, Enver Pasha, made a secret promise to support Germany and her allies. This alliance became public knowledge on 4 November 1914, when Ottoman ships bombarded Russia's port of Odessa. Two days later, British ships in the Arabian Gulf responded, by firing into the Shatt-al-Arab waterway in southern Mesopotamia (modern Iraq).

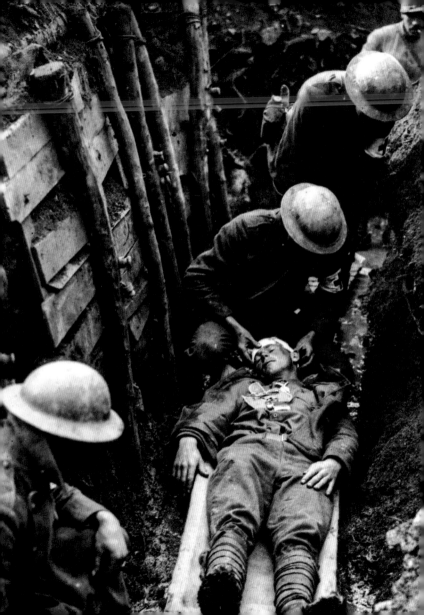

Life in the Trenches

By the beginning of 1915, the Western Front was dominated by trench warfare. Trenches varied with the landscape, but in general they were dug deep into the ground, with their walls shored up with boards and stakes. German trenches tended to be better positioned, more elaborate and more durable than those dug by the Allies. Behind the forward trenches stretched an intricate network of secondary and tertiary ones, and beyond these lay heavy artillery and a mass of infrastructure to support the men, machines and horses.

As the reality of this grim industrialized war began to bite, some military traditions were abandoned. The French Army abandoned the *pantalon rouge* in favour of the more discreet *horizon bleu* uniform, designed to merge into the skyline. Armies also adopted metal helmets, such as the French Adrian and the British Brodie. Both can be seen in this photograph, which shows a Red Cross team tending a head wound

Life in the trenches was frequently soggy and unhygienic. Men suffered with lice and rats, 'trench foot' and 'trench fever' and were fed on bland, repetitive rations including tinned or 'bully' beef.

The Artillery War

By 1915, twenty-five years of rapid military innovation had transformed the relationship between humans and artillery. By the outbreak of the First World War, massive guns could be deployed with previously unimaginable lethality, blasting out a relentless barrage of shrapnel shells, high explosives and even gas shells. As well as long-barrelled guns, the battlefields were plagued by howitzers – snub-nosed weapons that sent shells arcing high into the air before plummeting onto enemy gunnery, fortifications or trenches. A direct hit would obliterate virtually everything within a large radius.

The example shown here is a German 15cm *schwere Feldhaubitze*, or 'heavy field howitzer', concealed in a camouflaged placement to hide it from the eyes of enemy spotter planes. The artillerymen here are covering their ears, presumably in preparation to fire. Few soldiers on the Western Front ever forgot the cacophony of artillery bombardments, whose effects were a major cause of the post-traumatic stress disorder known as 'shell shock'.

The Shell Crisis

On 9 May 1915 a British attack on the Western Front, known as the Battle of Aubers Ridge, ended in unmitigated failure. In the aftermath, Sir John French, commander-in-chief of the British Expeditionary Force, complained bitterly to a journalist of *The Times* about the lack of high-explosive shells available to his artillery. The 'shell crisis' became a national scandal, and a new Ministry of Munitions – headed by the effervescent Welsh politician David Lloyd George – was created in order to oversee a massive increase in shell production.

The shell crisis had a profound impact on British society, as large numbers of women were called upon to produce the required ammunition. They were paid less than men, worked long hours, and some, particularly the shell-fillers, took their chances with toxic substances and accidental explosions. But their jobs provided income, welfare, food, sometimes housing, and a sense of community that many welcomed. Women's work during this war played an important role in the struggle for women's suffrage.

The Sinking of the *Lusitania*

On 1 May 1915, RMS *Lusitania*, a luxurious British passenger liner, departed New York bound for Britain with nearly 2,000 people aboard and a quantity of arms and ammunition in the cargo hold. The rules of war held that passenger liners should never be targeted by military vessels, but on 7 May, protocol was abandoned.

The *Lusitania* was in waters off the southern coast of Ireland when the German submarine *U-20* fired a torpedo. It found its mark in her hull, ripping a hole below the waterline and causing an internal explosion. *Lusitania* sank within twenty minutes of the attack, with the loss of 1,198 lives. They included most of the 139 Americans aboard, citizens of a neutral country. Those few bodies that were recovered – numbering around 300 – were buried in Ireland (as shown here), at mass funerals attended by hundreds of mourners. Although a tragic loss of civilian life, the sinking of the *Lusitania* was a major victory for Allied propaganda, which emphasized German viciousness and the illegality of the Kaiser's war.

Gallipoli

This beach on the Gallipoli peninsula in Turkey, now known as Anzac Cove, was the starting point of one of the most ignominious Allied land operations of the First World War.

Beginning on 19 February 1915, the Gallipoli campaign was meant to be a naval affair: to restore Russian access to the Mediterranean from the Black Sea and to menace Constantinople, the Ottoman capital. However, within weeks, it became clear that amphibious landings were needed to clear the threat from the shore. On 25 April 1915, thousands of troops, largely of the Australian and New Zealand Army Corps (ANZAC), disembarked on the sand. They were in for months of attritional uphill fighting until Allied troops were extracted by 9 January 1916.

Britain's First Lord of the Admiralty, Winston Churchill, lost his job as a result of Gallipoli. By contrast, the Turkish divisional commander Mustafa Kemal emerged as an Ottoman hero. In Australia and New Zealand, Gallipoli remains central to modern ideas about nationhood and remembrance.

Austria's Soldiers

Archduke Joseph Ferdinand of Austria (*right*), who also enjoyed the historic title of Duke of Tuscany, was a man steeped in Austrian military tradition. In 1915, he led the Austrian Fourth Army. But in an Austro-Hungarian Empire riven by competing nationalisms, multiple languages and superficial loyalties, it was an uphill struggle to imbue troops with a sense of cohesion and to maintain morale. In this propaganda photograph, the archduke is posing alongside thirteen-year-old Josef Kaswurm, from the Tyrol: the youngest soldier in imperial service.

Propaganda was needed, because as 1915 opened, Austria-Hungary's problems were multiplying. In launching weak attacks on both Serbia and Russia, the empire's armies had suffered more than 950,000 casualties. They had been driven out of Serbia, and Russia had counter-invaded Galicia (on the modern-day border between Poland and Ukraine), where the archduke was serving. Despite his empire's ailing fortunes during the First World War, the archduke survived. He eventually died in 1942, having endured a brief period in a Nazi concentration camp. Kaswurm's fate is unknown.

The Armenian Genocide

'An Armenian child lies dead in the fields within sight of help and safety at Aleppo.' This simple, awful caption written in faded typescript accompanies the original black-and-white photograph, which has been reproduced thousands of times to illustrate the cycle of violence widely known as the Armenian Genocide.

Tensions between Turks and Armenian Christians in eastern Anatolia had existed since the days of the medieval crusades. The poisonous circumstances of the First World War ensured that hundreds of years of ill feeling now boiled over. Early in 1915, the Ottoman Third Army was routed by Russian troops in the southern Caucasus. Many attributed the defeat to ethnic Armenians fighting – treacherously, in Turkish eyes – with the Russians.

In May 1915, an Ottoman government decree ordered the forcible removal of Turkey's Armenian population, many to Syria. During the deportations that followed, as many as one million Armenians died, from starvation, disease, violence, deprivation, neglect and exposure. The designation of 'genocide' is still hotly denied in Turkey. But the photographic legacy tells its own story.

Italy Enters the War

Italian mountain troops, known as the *Alpini*, had a long and distinguished history of service inside and outside Italy. The *Alpini* had fought in Abyssinia (Ethiopia and Eritrea) during Italy's attempts at colonial conquest in the 1880s and 1890s, and later in the Libyan desert. In 1915, however, they fought in one of the most punishing terrains of the First World War – the high-altitude *fronte alpino* (Alpine Front) on the border with Austria-Hungary.

Despite being a member of the pre-war Triple Alliance, with Germany and Austria-Hungary, the Italian government declined to join the fighting in the autumn of 1914. It was not until May 1915 that Italy was persuaded to enter the fray – on the Allied side, having been tempted by generous British war loans and the prospect of regaining territory around the north-eastern Adriatic known as *Italia irredenta* ('unredeemed Italy').

Belatedly called into service, the *Alpini* were soon busy doing what they did best: gouging out ice tunnels, climbing sheer rock faces, and risking falls and avalanches.

Flight from Serbia

Austro-Hungarian armies had invaded Serbia three times in 1914, and on each occasion had been beaten back. But, in late November 1915, faced by a joint assault of German, Austro-Hungarian and Bulgarian forces, the Serbian Army, together with its king, Peter I, and retinues of civilian followers, was forced into a long winter march towards the Adriatic coast, where survivors were evacuated to Corfu.

In the gruelling expedition, men, women and children starved or sickened, and one in ten of the 140,000-odd refugees died. The marchers were at the mercy of Albanian tribal attacks, too: memories of the ferocious Balkan wars fought earlier in the decade remained strong. A moment during the escape is captured in this photograph: Serbian soldiers march past what appears to be a shoe shop, watched by curious onlookers.

Meanwhile, the Serbian population faced a terrible wartime occupation. In relative terms, more Serbs died in this war than did citizens of any other fighting nation.

Poison Gas

Military scientists experimented with using poison gas against enemy troops on the Eastern Front; but its first major use on the battlefield came on 22 April 1915, when the Germans released more than 5,700 canisters of chlorine gas during the Second Battle of Ypres. Airborne chlorine scorched the lungs of those who inhaled it, causing panic as well as terrible internal injuries.

Using gas in warfare was officially considered an affront to humanity – the Hague Convention of 1899 had prohibited the 'diffusion of asphyxiating or deleterious gases'. But very quickly the efficiency of poison gas at disabling its victims led to its widespread use by all sides. Armies responded by scrambling to give their front-line troops protective equipment as a matter of course. At first, anti-gas kits consisted of goggles and face pads soaked in bicarbonate of soda – or urine. But by autumn 1915, prototypes of the respirator gas mask became available, as modelled by these German soldiers. The donkey 'wears' a human mask, but specialized equine masks also became available, in a war involving millions of horses.

Airship Attacks

In the first year of the Great War, it seemed as though all the nineteenth-century rules of conflict had been abandoned, as mass casualties proliferated and assaults on civilians were becoming normalized. Even Britons in their island homes were unsafe. The first bombardments of British civilians came from opportunistic battlecruisers, which shelled Great Yarmouth on 3 November 1914. But two months later, on 19 January 1915, the same Norfolk town became the first to be targeted by a new danger: airships.

Airship attacks were part of a deliberate German attempt to sap civilian morale. By night, hydrogen-filled dirigibles would release payloads of up to 1,360kg (3,000lb) of explosives onto towns below. On 31 May 1915, London was hit for the first time, when bombs fell across the East End and the north of the city, killing or injuring forty people.

Scenes of destruction, like the one photographed here, drew curious crowds, eager for a taste of 'real' war. Yet within a few months, airship attacks were old news. A more efficient aerial killer was emerging: bomber planes.

Attrition

At 7.00 a.m. on 1 July 1916, in a narrow British support trench opposite the little village of Beaumont Hamel in Picardy, northern France, a handful of men attempted a last few minutes of rest under cover. Around them, trench-digging had dispersed a white layer across this chalky landscape. As the men waited, John Warwick Brooke, a photographer attached to the Royal Engineers, caught a look in the eyes of one man – perhaps of trepidation, perhaps resignation or just plain weariness.

For a week, 1,400 Allied guns had rained artillery shells on the German lines opposite. At 7.20 a.m. on 1 July, the first of several gigantic mines under German positions was detonated, and finally, at 7.30 a.m. – Zero Hour – British and French infantry clambered out of their trenches to commence the assault.

For many of the British Tommies, this was their introduction to war. They had signed up in 'pals battalions', recruited from the same localities and workplaces. Now, they were on the Somme. The men advanced slowly, as instructed, rifles shouldered, heavy kit on their backs. They had been told that enemy trenches would have been obliterated. In fact, the bombardment had failed to destroy barbed wire or penetrate German bunkers. In the north of the sector, which included Beaumont Hamel, two waves of British soldiers were caught in the wire and massacred by machine guns. The attack was more successful further south, particularly for the French, but the British story was of unprecedented loss. On the first day of the Somme, 57,470 British servicemen died, went missing and or were wounded: the worst toll of casualties for any day in the British Army's history, before or since. Four months of bloody, grinding attrition lay ahead.

An Allied attack in this area had been planned since February 1916, as part of a new strategy of coordinated offensives. But its timing was thrown off when, on 21 February, thousands of German shells pounded the forests and forts around the French citadel of Verdun, beginning a titanic Franco-German struggle there. The British now agreed to shoulder the bulk of the Somme fighting, using 'New Armies' composed of men recruited since 1914. In many ways, they were unready for battle, and their commander-in-chief, Sir Alexander Haig, knew it. British and Imperial forces suffered the loss of more than 21,000 lives for every mile they advanced. The arrival of tanks on the Allied side, in September 1916, threw the German defenders into panic, but brought no decisive breakthroughs.

Beyond the Somme, the British war effort waxed and waned. A clash of naval fleets in the Battle of Jutland cost thousands of lives, and it was followed in June 1916 by the death at sea of War Secretary Earl Kitchener himself, whose call to arms had created the New Armies. A new but much more unorthodox national hero was emerging in the sands of the Middle East: T.E. Lawrence 'of Arabia'; but at Kut, on the other side of the Arabian peninsula, besieged Indian troops faced starvation and disease. The war fuelled violence in Ireland, where militant republicans tried to stage a revolution. And in August 1917, Haig began a Flanders offensive that would include the atrocious rain- and mud-filled Battle of Passchendaele, and which left hundreds of thousands more British, Imperial and German soldiers dead.

In Germany, general shock at the casualties caused by the Kaiser's war steadily increased. It was true that in many places the war had gone rather well for Germany in 1916–17: Italian defeat at Caporetto, the occupation of Romania, and revolutionary spirit sweeping Russia were all good news for the Central Powers. Yet the Western Front remained stubbornly mired.

On 23 December 1916, Haig described the Somme campaign as having been worth it 'to wear down the strength of the forces opposed to us'. The German general Otto von Below had demanded: 'only over corpses may the enemy find his way forward'. The cost of such military attitudes was captured by Wilfred Owen, who served at the Somme and distilled its horror in his poem 'Anthem for Doomed Youth'.

'What passing-bells for these who die as cattle?' he wrote. 'Only the monstrous anger of the guns.'

Verdun

The city of Verdun, on the River Meuse in northeastern France, had long experience of German aggression. It had been attacked in both Napoleonic times and during the Franco-Prussian War of 1870–71, so by the time of the First World War it was staunchly and massively defended. Unfortunately, its symbolism as a bulwark of French defence helped turn the land around Verdun into a slaughterhouse.

The Battle of Verdun began at 4 a.m. on 21 February 1916, when shells from 1,200 German guns exploded along a 25-mile (40km) front. Within four days, Verdun's largest fort, Douaumont, surrendered. For the next nine months, both sides approached the battle as warfare by attrition. The German aim was to try to bleed the French Army 'to death'. The French, for their part, adopted a strategy summarized by General Robert Nivelle: *Ils ne passeront pas!* ('They shall not pass!'). Verdun became the longest battle of the war, producing roughly 700,000 casualties, including a quarter of a million dead or missing. This lifeless German serviceman was just one of that grotesque number.

The Easter Rising

Britain's commitments to the world war had diverted attention from serious problems on the home front. In April 1916 these erupted, with a rebellion in Dublin against British rule in Ireland, which became known as the Easter Rising. The British government had agreed that full implementation of Home Rule would have to wait until the war was over. But not everyone was happy: particularly the members of the Irish Republican Brotherhood (IRB), who – with German backing – saw the war as an opportunity.

On Easter Monday, 24 April 1916, armed IRB revolutionaries gathered in central Dublin and marched on locations around the city, beginning a five-day battle with British forces. This photograph shows children clambering over a shattered street, which has been ruined by fighting that involved shells, machine-gun fire and grenades. More than 450 people died and fierce reprisals followed, in which the British executed fifteen rebel leaders by firing squad. But the swift revenge served to harden popular support for the Irish nationalist movement. Trouble between Britain and Ireland was a very long way from being over.

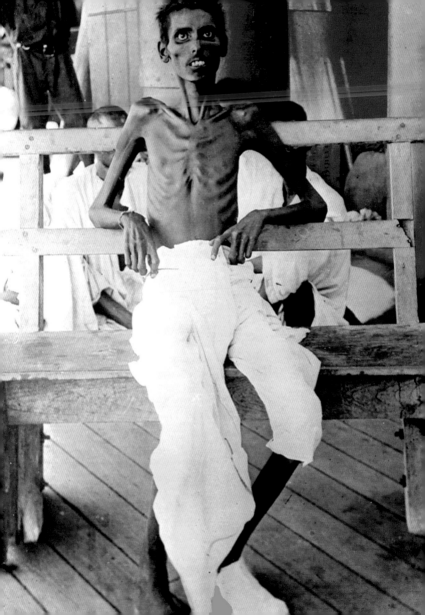

The Siege of Kut

Nearly 6,000km away from Dublin, in Mesopotamia, the spring of 1916 brought very different problems for Britain. Thousands of British and Indian troops were besieged by the Ottoman Army in the town of Kut. The siege began in December 1915, when troops were ordered by Major-General Sir Charles Townshend to take refuge in the town. There, they were pinned down by forces under the command of the notoriously brutal Turkish commander Halil Pasha and an elderly Prussian field marshal named Colmar Freiherr von der Goltz.

As attempts to relieve Kut proved futile, food and supplies failed. Eventually, on 29 April 1916, Townshend surrendered. He spent the rest of the war under house arrest, but his emaciated troops, like the Indian soldier photographed here, suffered far grimmer fates. Around 4,000 men died in captivity, some from disease and others from exhaustion.

For the Ottomans, this was a triumph. For the British, the siege of Kut was a debacle to compare with Gallipoli – and it was judged by many as the most abject Allied defeat of the entire war.

The Brusilov Offensive

On the Eastern Front in Europe, 1916 brought one of the deadliest and most dramatic military campaigns. It was carried out on the orders of Tsar Nicholas II, but named after his most brilliant general, Aleksei Brusilov. The aims were to respond to demoralizing Russian defeats in 1915 and 1916, to inflict catastrophic damage on the Austro-Hungarian Army, and to relieve pressure on Russia's allies on the Western and Italian fronts. The offensive began on 4 June 1916. Hundreds of thousands of prisoners were taken within the first week, and by the end of summer Brusilov had pushed all the way to the Carpathian mountains. Casualties were appalling on both sides, but the damage to the Austro-Hungarian Empire was ultimately fatal.

In this image, Tsar Nicholas is inspecting the troops destined for the Brusilov Offensive. Typically, they wear peaked caps – few Russian soldiers had helmets. To face the rigours of climate and terrain, the men carry greatcoats rolled up around their torsos, and wear high-quality black leather boots.

Kitchener's Farewell

On 1 June 1916, the sixty-five-year-old Field Marshal Lord (Horatio Herbert) Kitchener was photographed striding purposefully down the steps of Britain's War Office. Four days later, he was dead. Kitchener was on his way to a summit in Russia, when his ship collided with a German sea mine near Scapa Flow and sank. His body was never found.

Kitchener's death shocked the nation, for he was one of the British Empire's greatest celebrities. At the turn of the century he had made his reputation fighting in Sudan and South Africa; in August 1914 he had been appointed as Secretary of State for War, and he had rightly judged that Britain was destined for a war of far greater length and severity than most imagined. In light of this, Kitchener had urged a major military recruitment drive – lending his distinctive moustachioed countenance to posters calling on patriotic young Britons to sign up for service.

King George V called Kitchener's death 'a heavy blow to me and a great loss to the nation and the allies'.

Guns of the Somme

Although the Battle of the Somme officially began a month after Kitchener's death, on 1 July 1916, it was preceded by an Allied artillery barrage that lasted for seven days and rained around 1.7 million shells on German lines. Yet despite this monstrous battering, when British troops began their marches on enemy positions, they were mown down in their thousands by machine-gun fire.

This was the paradox of artillery on the Western Front. Despite the terror and the carnage that heavy shelling could cause, it was a blunt instrument that often failed in its purpose, generally serving as an alert to the enemy that an attack was imminent.

The British Army's largest guns were handled by the Royal Garrison Artillery (RGA). This photograph, taken in August 1916 during the Somme offensive, shows the RGA's 39th Siege Battery in action on the chalky terrain of the Fricourt–Mametz valley. They are firing 8-inch heavy howitzers: these were considered a reliable workhorse gun, and were often used to try to knock out enemy artillery and infrastructure.

Romania's Conqueror

One of the most striking and experienced officers in the German Army, Field Marshal August von Mackensen was a veteran of wars stretching back to the 1870s. Aged sixty-four at the outbreak of the First World War, he had earned much of his vast military experience in Prussian Hussar regiments, and thus the right to wear the black *Totenkopf* (death's head) uniform, complete with fur busby, in which he is photographed here. In 1914 and 1915, Mackensen had commanded armies with great distinction on the Eastern Front and against Serbia. In 1916, he had a new prey in his sights: Romania.

Romania declared war on Austria-Hungary in August 1916. In response, Mackensen was sent into Romania with a multinational army including German, Ottoman, Austro-Hungarian and Bulgarian units, capturing Bucharest by December. The Kaiser awarded him the highest class of the Iron Cross and named a new battleship class after him. In 1917, Mackensen was appointed as the military governor of occupied Romania and survived long beyond the end of the First World War. He lived until 1945, when he was ninety-five.

Tanks

While Mackensen was rampaging through Romania, the Somme campaign continued to devour lives, money and military attention. As it did so, new technologies were deployed to try to break the deadlock. On 15 September 1916, at the Battle of Flers-Courcelette, the British Army unleashed tanks onto the battlefield for the first time.

Fighting in these early tanks was difficult and dangerous. To begin with, crews rode next to the engine and fuel tank – which was only moved outside the body of the vehicle with the development of the Mark IV tank, seen here crossing an old trench in 1917. Tanks could be damaged by heavy machine-gun fire and artillery, were difficult to steer, moved at a crawl, often broke down and relied (at least at first) on semaphore or even carrier pigeon for communications. But they offered the British commander Field Marshal Sir Douglas Haig significant psychological advantage on the battlefield, striking fear into the enemy and earning a reputation on the German side as 'devil's coaches'.

Lawrence of Arabia

In 1909, while studying history at Oxford University, Thomas Edward Lawrence – better known as T.E. Lawrence, or Lawrence of Arabia – embarked on a three-month, 1,000-mile walking tour of the medieval crusader castles of Syria. After graduating, he returned east, learned Arabic and became an archaeologist.

When war broke out, Lawrence was readily co-opted by British military intelligence and tasked with mapping the Negev desert. By 1916, Lawrence was in Arabia, building a friendship with Faisal, son of the grand Sharif of Mecca, and fomenting Arab Revolt against Ottoman rule. He dressed the part, too. Before long, Lawrence was more than just a British military liaison: he was effectively a guerrilla leader, and during the following two years his irregular forces attacked Ottoman railways and bridges and participated in the campaign to take Damascus, ending the war with rank of full colonel.

After the war, Lawrence became a celebrity, famous for his lectures, writing and exotic tales of derring-do. He joined the Royal Air Force in the 1920s, but died in a motorcycle accident in 1935.

The February Revolution

On the Western Front, the winter of 1916–17 finally brought to an end the bloody battles on the Somme and at Verdun. In the east, however, it ushered in a revolution that would change Russia forever. Russian success stalled after the Brusilov Offensive, and as it did so a sense of despondency deepened among ordinary Russians. Their anger was aimed at the man who had taken command of the war effort in 1915: Tsar Nicholas II.

This photograph, taken in Petrograd, shows workers from the Putilov metal plant during pay strikes, which began on 22 February 1917 (7 March, New Style). Strikes led to demonstrations in the streets. Within a week, the tsarist government had lost control, and workers and soldiers began forming their own authorities known as 'soviets'. On 2 March (15 March, New Style), Nicholas abdicated and his brother, Grand Duke Mikhail, refused the throne. A Provisional Government was formed to try and save the empire and continue the war. But Russia's revolution was far from over.

БРАТЬЯ МОРИ
БРАТЬ
ИБАВКУ ПАИКА
ЕМЬЯМЪ СОЛДАТЪ
АЩИТНИКАМЪ СВОБОДЫ
НАРОДНОГО МІРА.

The Air War

The Prussian aristocrat Manfred von Richthofen (*centre*), known as The Red Baron, was one of the most famous warriors produced by any side in the First World War. Handsome and deadly, he was all the more alluring because his weapon of choice was one that had been created by the war itself: the fighter plane.

At the start of the war, planes were primarily used for spying. However, the effectiveness of air reconnaissance prompted the invention of aircraft purposed to shoot down enemy planes; and in 1915, German engineers developed machine guns that could be synchronized to fire through frontal propellers. From this point on, men like von Richthofen, standing here with fellow fighter pilots in front of a Fokker biplane, gripped the public's imagination.

The Red Baron was the British Royal Flying Corps' nemesis during a British offensive at Arras in 1917. During 'Bloody April', the British lost more than 200 planes to superior German tactics and technology. Von Richthofen survived the battle and was not killed for another year, until he was shot down in Vaux-sur-Somme and died muttering the word '*kaputt*'.

The Women's Reserve Ambulance

The general and widespread carnage of the First World War made plenty of work for women's volunteer organizations. One of these, active between 1915 and 1919, was the Women's Reserve Ambulance (WRA) Corps, also known as the Green Cross Corps. The WRA adopted khaki, battlefield-style clothing, wore felt hats and carried military ranks. They had mascots too: in this photograph, taken in June 1916, that role is played by a bulldog.

The WRA was an offshoot of the Women's Volunteer Reserve, founded in 1914 by Evelina Haverfield, an aristocratic suffragette from a military family. Much of the WRA's work would take place around Victoria Station in London, where its members met wounded soldiers coming home by train, as well as thousands of men on leave, whom they helped to find places to stay. Often part-timers, juggling family commitments, the women of the WRA took on a huge range of other tasks, too: assisting in the aftermath of airship raids, working as orderlies in hospitals, and transporting munitions.

Caporetto

The autumn of 1917 was a decisive time on the Italian Front, since it brought to an end the long series of twelve battles along the Isonzo River, which had raged ever since Italy entered the war in 1915. This photograph, which shows dead Italian soldiers carpeting the rocky hillside near Cividale, illustrates the ferocity with which those engagements were fought.

By the late summer of 1917, it had become clear that both the Italian and Austro-Hungarian forces fighting along the Isonzo were exhausted. Kaiser Wilhelm approved the transfer of German divisions to join the fight against the demoralized Italians. On 24 October, a gas attack and artillery bombardment at Caporetto (now Kobarid, in Slovenia) announced the beginning of the final battle of the Isonzo. As further German and Austro-Hungarian troops poured forward, their attacks produced a collapse in the whole Italian line and a chaotic retreat. Italian soldiers threw away their uniforms and deserted, while hundreds of thousands of others simply surrendered. It was a bloody, humiliating disaster that would live long and bitter in Italian national memory.

Passchendaele

While Italian forces were crushed at Caporetto, another notorious battle was taking place on the Western Front. There was fighting around the Belgian city of Ypres throughout the First World War, but it was never more miserable than during the phase known as the Battle of Passchendaele.

In mid-July 1917, British guns fired four million shells towards German lines in preparation for an infantry attack. All this did was plough the clay soil of these Flanders fields; and when torrential rain began early, in August, the ground became a thick, sapping quagmire. This British stretcher party (photographed near Boesinghe, a few miles from Passchendaele) was already knee-deep on 1 August.

The British and Imperial soldiers who took part in the three-month offensive in this foul marsh remembered hideous privations: men and horses drowning in mud; troops caught in barbed wire and machine-gunned to death; men dying mad from the horror. They ultimately gained 5 miles (8km) of territory at the cost of a total 475,000 casualties across all sides. 'I died in hell', wrote the poet Siegfried Sassoon. 'They called it Passchendaele.'

The Ruins of Ypres

The three great battles of Ypres, of which the third encompassed Passchendaele, left the city devastated, as this aerial photograph taken after the worst of the fighting shows. At the centre of this picture are the ruins of the medieval St Martin's Church. To the right is the burnt-out Cloth Hall, another great Gothic construction dating to the Middle Ages. Towards the top of the image is the so-called Plaine d'Amour or Minneplein, a grassy area that was redeployed as a cemetery.

British servicemen called Ypres 'Wipers' and published a satirical newspaper, *The Wipers Times*, produced on a printing press that had been abandoned by a fleeing Belgian publisher. The first issue of this newssheet, dated 12 February 1916, compared Ypres' 'jagged spires' to 'the fingers of ghosts' that 'seem to point to heaven, crying for vengeance'.

After the end of the war, Ypres was rebuilt, with the great medieval buildings returned as closely as possible to their former splendour. Ypres is today the location of the Menin Gate memorial, which commemorates the graveless British and Imperial dead.

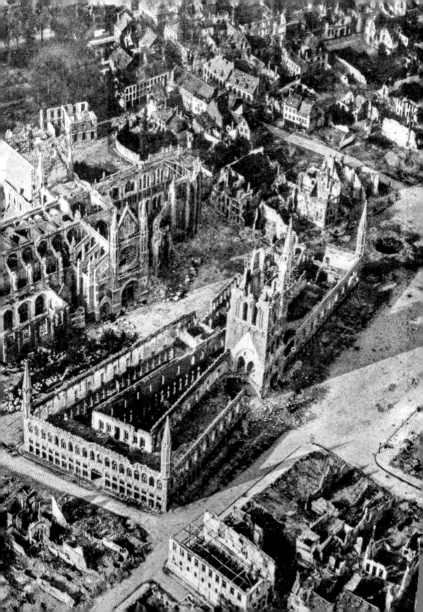

Breakthrough

Corporal Fred McIntyre (*left*) served in the First World War with the 369th Infantry Regiment of the US Army – a regiment better known by their nickname, the 'Harlem Hellfighters'. To his fellow Hellfighters, McIntyre was known as a 'Devil's Man'. But American entry into the war was viewed by many on the Allied side as far from diabolical.

At the outbreak of war, the US government had been reluctant to engage – reflecting a strong strain of American public opinion favouring pacifism and neutrality. Nevertheless, stories of German atrocities and the 'rape of Belgium' became harder to discount. So too were German attacks on American ships, especially when, on 1 February 1917, Germany renewed a policy of 'unrestricted' U-boat attacks, putting the vessels of neutral nations at risk. Then, in February 1917, President Woodrow Wilson learned of the so-called Zimmermann Telegram whereby Germany scouted out an alliance with Mexico on the understanding that Mexico would 'reconquer her lost territory in Texas, New Mexico and Arizona'. Public outrage now overtook isolationism. On 6 April, Wilson declared war on Germany, to make 'the world safe for democracy'.

So it was that in December 1917 the Hellfighters embarked for Europe, part of a surge that would send around two million Americans across the Atlantic before the war was over. The Hellfighters, formed from the New York National Guard, were remarkable for several reasons: their uncommon valour; their exceptional, ragtime-influenced regimental band; and their blackness. Only 10 per cent of US servicemen were African-Americans, and just two 'Colored' divisions were permitted to bear arms – a consequence of the enduring, wretched racism of American society and a deep fear on the part of white America at giving military training to descendants of slaves.

By July 1918, the 369th was fighting alongside the French on the River Marne. Indeed, for military purposes they had actually become French, since they had been seconded to the French Army. They fought for longer – and suffered more casualties – than any other American regiment in the war, and they were highly decorated for their bravery. One of their number, Henry 'Black Death' Porter, was the first American to be awarded the prestigious French Croix de Guerre – an award subsequently bestowed on the whole 369th. McIntyre was photographed when the Hellfighters returned home to New York and a hero's welcome, in 1919, aboard the USS *Stockholm*. He had taken his picture of the Kaiser, framed with bullets, from a German soldier and thereafter carried it for good luck.

American entry into the First World War contrasted vividly with Russia's exit, amid the shake-up of a Bolshevik revolution.

That turmoil prompted a vicious civil war in neighbouring Finland, as it broke off from the Russian Empire. In March 1918, Russia signed the Treaty of Brest-Litovsk and quit the European war on terms heavily favourable to Germany and the other Central Powers.

Russia's crises should have been a boon to the Ottoman Empire, yet the Turks ended 1917 in disarray, having lost much ground to a combination of British Imperial forces and Arab irregulars. In December, British forces captured Jerusalem, and General Edmund Allenby entered the city on foot, an event that was celebrated in some quarters – despite official British disapproval – as the culmination of a 'new crusade'.

For Germany, the space between Russia's collapse and America's meaningful presence on the battlefield offered a window for a final, major push for victory. The Spring Offensive, or *Kaiserschlacht*, of 1918 gained more territory on the Western Front than had been taken by any side since the first months of the war. But German efforts ultimately proved futile. The Allied counter-attack, known as the Hundred Days Offensive, succeeded in reversing Germany's springtime gains.

The only serious question left was how German surrender would be framed. It was answered with the Armistice, which came into force at 11 a.m. on 11 November 1918. The last serviceman on the Allied side to die in action was US Sergeant Henry Gunther, gunned down while charging enemy lines one minute before peace was officially declared. He was one of around 54,000 US soldiers killed during their brief involvement in the most terrible war the world had ever known.

Liberty Loans

Roscoe 'Fatty' Arbuckle was a popular and highly paid Hollywood star of comic 'two-reeler' movies. Here, he is pasting up a poster in New York's Times Square, rallying the American public for the 'Second Liberty Loan of 1917'. Arbuckle was not alone in lending his weight to this campaign: fellow film stars Charlie Chaplin, Douglas Fairbanks and Mary Pickford also encouraged Americans to help their government bankroll Allied efforts in the First World War.

Between April 1917 and September 1918, the US Treasury issued four series of war bonds, initially aimed at big investors but later at ordinary people. In theory, these bonds paid out a guaranteed interest rate, beginning at 3.5 per cent, and buyers would be able to redeem them after fifteen years. To whip up enthusiasm for the scheme, the euphemistically titled Committee on Public Information was charged with mobilizing public opinion and cultivating a general sense of patriotic obligation. The slogan of one typical poster left no ambiguity: 'Your Duty – Buy United States Government Bonds'.

London's Mighty Welcome

On 15 August 1917, London witnessed an extraordinary scene. Hundreds of young American soldiers marched, four abreast, through St James's Park, past the US Embassy, where they gave a salute, and on to Buckingham Palace. There King George V, accompanied by Queen Alexandra and Prime Minister David Lloyd George, took another salute. Around the snaking column thronged thousands of Londoners, including this small child, who joined hands with one of the 'Doughboys', as American infantrymen were known. Government newsreels called the parade 'London's Mighty Welcome'.

And welcome they were. US entry into the war promised money, resources, ammunition, and an enormous supply of manpower for a conflict in which brute force and sheer numbers mattered so much. Yet in 1917 the US Army was one of the smallest of all the nations at war. A mass draft was introduced, but it could not manufacture the necessary military experience. Months of training and acclimatization to the Western Front lay ahead.

Trotsky

Leon Trotsky – a Ukrainian whose real name was Lev Davidovich Bronstein – was an experienced revolutionary. Like all Russia's Marxist-inspired 'Social Democrats', he opposed the First World War and Russia's involvement in it. During the first three years of war, he led a nomadic existence before expulsion from various European countries took him to the United States. After the February Revolution of 1917, Trotsky saw an opportunity to return home.

By the summer, the Russian Army was mutinying on a massive scale, yet the government staggered on. Trotsky found himself in jail again following the violent demonstrations in Petrograd known as the 'July Days'. However, in prison Trotsky fell in with the Bolshevik Party and joined its central committee. His moment had come.

By the time this photograph of Trotsky was taken in the Georgian city of Sukhumi in early 1924, the Bolsheviks were in control of Russia. However, his ally, Lenin, was dead and Trotsky was falling out of favour. He was about to be rejected (and eventually exiled and murdered) by the regime he had done so much to create.

The Winter Palace

In October 1917, Russia's Provisional Government collapsed under a revolution led by the Bolshevik Party. It took place over forty-eight hours, between 25 and 26 October [7–8 November, New Style], as insurgents occupied government buildings across Petrograd. Overnight, revolutionaries overran the government's headquarters at the former Tsar's Winter Palace. It was not an especially violent siege; the defending troops either slunk away or were ordered to stand down. But there was damage throughout the building – as photographs like this one, of the chamber known as the 'Tsar Alexander II Cabinet', record.

Russia was now to be radically and bloodily reconstituted under Bolshevik rule, with Lenin (born Vladimir Ilyich Ulyanov) the head of government. On 3 March 1918, in the Treaty of Brest-Litovsk, the Bolshevik government traded peace with the Central Powers for the loss of Ukraine, Belarus, Poland, the Baltic states and more, along with huge coal reserves. Their world war was over. A civil war now loomed.

The War on Hunger

Dwindling food supplies and straitened conditions for ordinary people were acute in Russia. But in Britain, too, wartime conditions were beginning to bite. By late 1917, food shortages combined with rising prices led to queues outside shops, as people competed for goods they could barely afford. One response aimed at helping those struggling to survive was state-sponsored canteens. The one shown here is in Bow, in London's East End. Smartly dressed staff and trained cooks served up no-frills, inexpensive but nutritious dishes to diners who bought a ticket and lined up to make their choices.

In early 1918, the government introduced food rationing across the country. Basic staples including bread, margarine, meat, flour, butter and sugar were therefore only made available on presentation of ration cards. This policy, along with the introduction of naval convoys to protect merchant shipping, helped keep Britain fed. In this respect, Britons were significantly better off than their German, Russian, Austro-Hungarian and Turkish counterparts, who suffered malnutrition and in many cases starvation.

The Battle of Cambrai

At the end of 1917, the British public was greeted with exciting news of the Battle of Cambrai. This was an extraordinary engagement for several reasons: first because it represented the first mass tank attack in history, and second because the British punctured, albeit briefly, the long German defensive position known as the Hindenburg Line (*Siegfriedstellung*).

On 20 November, the British assault slammed through the German defences, along a 10-mile (16km) front, making gains that were spectacular. But momentum soon ran out. Ten days after the battle began, the German Second Army, led by General Georg von der Marwitz, turned the tables, halting the British advance with attacks along their flanks, and using fast-moving stormtroopers to 'infiltrate' and to isolate heavily defended strongpoints. By the beginning of December, the Hindenburg Line had been more or less restored, and the Germans had seized around thirty damaged Mark IV tanks for their own use. Imitation, in this case, was the sincerest form of flattery.

The Fall of Jerusalem

On 11 December 1917, General Edmund Allenby marched on foot through the Jaffa Gate of Jerusalem's Old City, to take control of it in the name of the Egyptian Expeditionary Force and the British Empire. The capture of Jerusalem was a boon for the British and a bane for the Ottoman Empire and its German allies. The Ottomans had already surrendered much ground in Palestine and had suffered defeats at Gaza, Jaffa, Beersheba and elsewhere; eventually, the governor of Jerusalem had surrendered the city for fear that 'deadly bombs will hit the holy places' – shrines on the Temple Mount (Haram al-Sharif) and elsewhere.

In this picture, Allenby (*front row, third from right*) is flanked by colonels Philpin de Piépape and Francesco d'Agostino, commanders of the small French and Italian detachments respectively. Further right is François Georges-Picot, who would represent French interests in reshaping the Middle East. Not visible, but present, was T. E. Lawrence, who called this day the pinnacle of his war.

Spanish Flu

By 1918, the First World War had caused as many as 20 million deaths. At least as many people again would die in one of the worst pandemics in world history, which began during the last year of the war. 'Spanish' flu did not begin in Spain: the name stemmed from the fact that this neutral country's press openly discussed the disease, whereas the belligerents in the war censored newspaper reporting for fear of damaging public morale. Wherever its origins, the flu was lethal, causing a sharp, wracking cough and a soaring fever, along with bleeding from the ears and lungs. Death could be very rapid, within twenty-four hours of symptoms showing, or could result from a secondary infection of pneumonia.

Despite scrambled attempts by health agencies worldwide to control the spread of Spanish flu, it peaked in the last three months of 1918, when this photograph demonstrating flu protocols was taken at the US Red Cross Ambulance Station in Washington, D.C. By the time the outbreak subsided, barely any part of the globe had remained untouched by it.

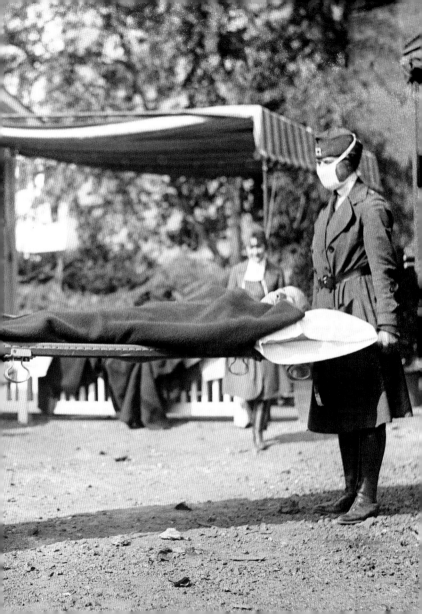

Prisoners of War

Besides monstrous numbers of killed and wounded, the First World War also produced around ten million captives. POW camps were therefore a regular sight behind the front lines. This German photograph shows captured soldiers of eight nationalities: 'Anamite [i.e. Vietnamese], Tunese [i.e. Tunisian] Senegalese, Sudanese, Russian, American, Portuguese, and English'.

This diversity among captives was hardly surprising. Britain's war effort alone had drawn in Indians and Canadians, Australians and New Zealanders, and men from the Caribbean and South Africa. German propaganda deplored this broad-based recruitment and railed against the deployment of 'savage' dark-skinned fighters, especially African Americans and men from sub-Saharan Africa fighting for the French. The composition of this photograph, in which subjects are arranged from the short 'Anamite' to the tall Englishman, reflects a mentality of racial and national grading; yet it also reveals how global the Western Front itself had become.

The Finnish Civil War

The collapse of the Russian monarchy and the rise of Bolshevism brought considerable trouble to Finland, which, for more than a century, had been a grand duchy within the Russian Empire. In December 1917, a Finnish declaration of independence heralded a vicious civil war. On one side were the 'Reds': leftists, urban-dwellers, workers, Russian-speakers, pro-Slavs and some remnants of the Russian Army. On the other were the 'Whites': an alliance of landowners, business owners, Swedish Finns, monarchist-conservatives, pro-Germans and the agricultural poor.

On 27 January, Red Guard paramilitaries staged a revolution in Helsinki, which began the war. They had some success for a month, but soon the amateur nature of Red leadership began to tell. The White forces were better equipped and reinforced by detachments of the German Army. This photograph shows Red fighters being marched through Helsinki as prisoners. By mid-May, the Whites had won the war.

Around 37,000 people had been killed, and horrifying memories of the war in this small country haunted Finnish society for generations.

The Spring Offensive

As Russia abandoned the First World War, and the United States prepared to join the Allied effort, the spring of 1918 represented the last possible opportunity for German victory. Beginning on 21 March, the *Kaiserschlacht* ('Kaiser's Battle') or Spring Offensive was built around five major attacks along the Western Front. The first and largest was known as 'Operation Michael', which surged across old battlefields of the Somme. Within a week 40 miles (64km) were gained. Vast, long-range Krupp siege guns bombarded Paris, and panic gripped the French capital at the thought that the city might fall.

Other German attacks hammered British and French positions in Flanders, the Aisne and the Marne. But by the early summer it was clear that the *Kaiserschlacht* had exhausted German fighting capability and created new bulges in the lines that were difficult to defend. American troops were arriving in ever-larger numbers, and a major Allied counter-attack (the 'Hundred Days Offensive') was about to begin. The end was in sight.

Marshal Foch

Ferdinand Foch had established a reputation as a charismatic, hyper-aggressive general early in the war, and on 26 March 1918, with German forces apparently scything towards Paris, he was appointed *Généralissime*: Supreme General of the Allied Armies. His mission was simple, if daunting: to halt the German advance, then win the war in the west.

Throughout a perilous and bloody spring and summer, Foch saw through his objective. The turning point came at the Second Battle of the Marne in July 1918, in which a major German advance was stopped in its tracks and Allied infantry, tanks and aircraft began a devastating counter-attack. As reward for his command, he was awarded the style 'Marshal of France' and a ceremonial baton bearing the Latin legend *Terror belli, decus pacis*: 'terror in war, ornament in peace'.

After the war, Foch was fêted and honoured around the world. When he died in 1929, he was entombed at Les Invalides, alongside other great French military leaders including Napoléon Bonaparte.

Pershing's Crusaders'

When US President Woodrow Wilson declared war in April 1917, his country was in no fit state to fight a world war. But by the summer of 1918, Americans were arriving on the Western Front at a rate of 10,000 a day. The overall leader of the American Expeditionary Forces (AEF) was General John J. Pershing, nicknamed 'Black Jack'.

The AEF's first major, independent success came on 12–15 September, when Pershing personally commanded an attack by the US First Army on German positions at a salient around the town of Saint-Mihiel, not far from Verdun. In pouring rain, aided by artillery, tanks and bomber aircraft, Pershing's troops hunted down retreating German forces and secured the salient. Despite their relative inexperience, US soldiers acquired a reputation with the Allies for almost reckless courage; and at home a postwar film celebrated them as 'Pershing's Crusaders'.

This photograph was taken near Saint-Mihiel the day after the battle was won. It shows Lieutenant-Colonel R.D. Garrett, signal officer in the 42nd 'Rainbow Division', wearing a British-style Brodie helmet as he tests a captured German field telephone.

The Hundred Days Offensive

The campaign that won the First World War began on 8 August 1918, with the first day of the Battle of Amiens: 550 British tanks took part, and by the time the battle was won, 30,000 German troops had surrendered.

Later known as the Hundred Days Offensive, the campaign reversed all the German gains from the Spring Offensive, punched holes in the Hindenburg Line and prompted rioting and revolution in German cities. After all their exertions since March, the German armies were low on supplies and haemorrhaging men. Meanwhile, millions of US troops were bolstering the Allied advance.

This picture of a dead German machine gunner, taken by Lieutenant M. S. Lentz, a photographer in the US Army Signal Corps, was captured late in the campaign, on 4 November 1918. The Allied success, the failure of the Hindenburg Line and the general collapse in German morale both on the Western Front and at home was enough to convince the German high command that the war was now unwinnable. On 9 November, the Kaiser abdicated. Two days later, the war was over.

Armistice

On 11 November 1918, an Armistice agreed in Marshal Foch's private train near Compiègne came into effect. By this date, Germany was fighting alone; the other Central Powers had already sued for peace between 29 September and 3 November. The Armistice – signed at 5 a.m. and executed at 11 a.m. – ordered an immediate halt to fighting, the withdrawal of German troops from occupied territories and the release of prisoners. The exact terms of peace were left to the later political conferences.

On the front lines, news of the Armistice was greeted with mixed emotions; even the twenty-four hours before it had brought 10,000 casualties. This photograph, taken the day after, shows two British officers – Captain Paget MC and 2nd Lieutenant Barry MC – reading out its terms to men of the 1st Battalion, Irish Guards Regiment, who were in a celebratory mood. They were at Maubeuge, less than 10 miles (16km) south of Mons, where some of them had fought in the first, desperate British battle with the Germans on 23 August 1914.

The Lost Generation

1919–1929

I n the summer of 1918, the writer F. Scott Fitzgerald, commissioned as a 2nd lieutenant in the US Army, was in Montgomery, Alabama, awaiting deployment to France. There he met his wife-to-be. Zelda Sayre, the youngest daughter of a well-to-do southern family, was also a dancer, a smoker, a drinker and a flirt, and her vivacious spirit was exemplary of the age that was unfolding. They married in 1920 and Zelda gave birth to their only child, Frances ('Scottie'), in 1921. This Christmas photograph was taken a few years later; by this time, Fitzgerald had been discharged from the army and had begun chronicling the era in novels including *This Side of Paradise*, *The Beautiful and Damned* and *The Great Gatsby*.

The world that the Fitzgeralds inhabited and – in a sense – created had been profoundly shaped by the First World War. For well-heeled Americans and Europeans, the 1920s oozed hedonism: a devil-may-care cocktail of jazz, parties, flapper dresses and art deco sheen, all helped by a bullish US economy. It was the 'Roaring Twenties' or the 'Jazz Age'. Behind this glamorous exterior, however, lurked troubles, including personal ones for the Fitzgeralds, whose marriage was plagued by drink, fights and jealousies, and by serious mental and physical health issues as well as financial woes.

Such contrasts between exterior glamour and underlying strife became themes for the artists and writers of the 1920s, many of whom – including the Fitzgeralds – congregated in Paris. A key figure in that circle was Gertrude Stein, writer and art collector, who coined the term 'lost generation' for this group's collective character: without a compass, moral or otherwise, caught between cynicism about American self-confidence and displacement in a war-weary Europe.

It was in Paris, too, where post-war Europe – and the world – was shaped, when its most powerful leaders gathered there in 1919 to thrash out peace terms. The resulting Treaty of Versailles – and a series of separate treaties imposed on the defeated powers – redrew boundaries, broke up empires, established new nations, and assigned responsibility for the damage done by the First World War. It was neither easy nor perfectly executed, as events would quickly prove.

In Germany, the abdication of Kaiser Wilhelm left a vacuum eventually filled by a tenuous republican government based in Weimar. It was hamstrung by the severe terms of Versailles, which included onerous reparation payments. Violence in the industrial Ruhr followed, as well as revolutionary agitation by political firebrands, including a war veteran called Adolf Hitler.

Further east, the Bolshevik coup that had created Soviet Russia was tested almost to the limit during the Russian Civil

War, while an attendant famine killed more Russians than the fighting of 1914–17. At the same time, the Austro-Hungarian Empire was broken up, creating newly independent states, and Poland – partitioned for more than a century – achieved statehood again. Polish independence owed much to Józef Piłsudski, a war hero and authoritarian strongman of a type that would become increasingly familiar, not least in the form of the Italian, Benito Mussolini: in 1922 his fascist thugs marched on Rome, and Mussolini was on his way to becoming Italy's dictatorial 'Duce'.

While imperial break-up was the order of the day for the defeated empires, it was a different story for the winning side. Admittedly, Britain was forced to grant self-government to Ireland – a process that led to partition on the island of Ireland and a bloody civil war – but in Africa and the Middle East, the British and French were ascendant, asserting their rights to administer former German and Ottoman colonies. But serious revolts in Syria and Palestine showed that the ruled were not always happy at the way their new colonial rulers wielded power.

Not all the post-war revolutions brought hardship: as a direct consequence of the First World War, women won the vote in many European countries and the USA. Overall, though, it is hard not to view the 1920s as an age of extremes. Between the hedonism of the Jazz Age and the cracked fields of famine-struck Russia, everything was in flux. 'I'm not sure about good and evil at all any more', reflected Fitzgerald's Amory Blaine in *This Side of Paradise*. He was not alone.

German Revolution

Kaiser Wilhelm II abdicated two days before the Armistice that ended the First World War, on the morning of 9 November 1918. On the same day, two socialist republics were declared in Germany: one by the moderate Social Democratic Party (SPD) and another by the radical *Spartakusbund*, or Spartacus League, whose leader, the lawyer and anti-war agitator Karl Liebknecht, announced his revolution from the balcony of the City Palace in Berlin, the building photographed here. From this confused state of affairs emerged an interim government, in which the SPD allied with military and right-wing militias to try to keep Germany from dissolving into full, Russian-style communist revolution.

This was not easy. The damage to the palace seen here was done during a skirmish between leftist sailors and army units on Christmas Eve 1918. By the end of January 1919, a semblance of order had been restored. Elections returned deputies to a new National Assembly, held in the city of Weimar. The SPD leader, Friedrich Ebert, was confirmed as president. But Germany was far from settled, and the wounds of the war would be a very long time healing.

The Treaty of Versailles

While Germans struggled to form a new internal government, the broader fate of the nation was being decided by the victorious powers. In January 1919 the leaders of Britain, France, the United States and Italy gathered to negotiate a treaty that formally ended the war. By 28 June this treaty was ready, and the Palace of Versailles's Hall of Mirrors was packed with dignitaries to witness its signing: the scene captured here.

Germany was denied a negotiating hand at Versailles, and as a result suffered extreme humiliation. Germany lost her empire, iron and coal resources were halved, and the German military was reduced to 100,000 volunteers and a token navy, without submarines. Most contentious was a 'war guilt' clause, which explicitly blamed Germany for causing the war, and in turn justified the imposition of financial reparations set at a staggering 132 billion gold marks (£6.6bn). It was a punishment that invited resentment and revenge, as a few wise heads realized at the time.

Women's Suffrage

The peace of 1918–19 redrew the political map of the world and the basic principles on which many nations were founded. Almost inadvertently, conflict and its aftermath had aided the struggle for women's suffrage. Across the West, women had played a critical role in the war, and as post-war reconstruction began, they were granted new freedoms. In Britain, women over thirty were granted the vote in 1918. Female suffrage became an important feature of the revolutions convulsing Germany and Austria in 1919. Poland, newly reconstituted, allowed women to vote in its very first elections.

In this photograph, women and girls in New York City hold a 'jubilee' to celebrate the ratification of the 19th Amendment to the US Constitution. 'The right of citizens of the United States to vote shall not be denied or abridged by the United States or by any State on account of sex,' it read. President Woodrow Wilson had taken his nation into war in 1917 on the understanding that he was making the world 'safe for democracy'. The time had come to keep the promise at home too.

New Faces

Hundreds of thousands of veterans returned from the front lines of the First World War mentally and physically traumatized. Many were left to deal with their problems alone – but not all. One extraordinary woman who helped return some appearance of normality to veterans was Anna Coleman Ladd.

Ladd was a portrait artist and sculptor who moved to Paris from her home in Massachusetts towards the end of the war when her husband, a doctor, was posted to France with the Red Cross. In 1918 she opened a studio in which she turned her artistic skills to the task of 'repairing' wounded soldiers' disfigured faces by creating lifelike prosthetic masks. This photograph gives some sense of Ladd's delicate craft, as she carefully paints skin tones onto a mask for one Monsieur Caudron. The limitations of the copper and enamel masks, with their fixed expressions, were obvious. But in helping to gain social acceptability for the patient, this was work that transformed lives.

Irish Civil War

The end of the world war did not bring calm to Ireland. Nationalist sentiment had intensified in the years since the Easter Rising of 1916, and, following post-war British elections that gave the republican party, Sinn Féin, a huge majority in Ireland, in January 1919 a revolutionary Irish parliament (the Dáil) declared independence. By September, Sinn Féin and the paramilitary Irish Republican Army (IRA) had been declared illegal by the British government and a vicious guerrilla war had broken out.

The Anglo-Irish Treaty that ended this war in December 1921 took the momentous step of partitioning Ireland between an Irish Free State with self-governing dominion status (like Canada or Australia) and Northern Ireland, composed of six of Ulster's nine counties, which remained part of the UK. Yet violence continued. In the summer of 1922, a civil war broke out in the Irish Free State between pro- and anti-treaty factions. The men pictured here near O'Connell Bridge in Dublin are members of the hastily recruited, pro-treaty Free State Army. Backed by the British, they fought against the IRA in a bloody struggle that lasted until May 1923.

Józef Piłsudski

Under the treaties that concluded the First World War, Poland, partitioned since the eighteenth century, was revived as a sovereign state. Responsibility for recreating the nation was entrusted to Józef Piłsudski.

In his youth, Piłsudski had been a dissident; as a medical student in the 1880s, he was exiled to Siberia for his supposed connection to a plot to kill the Russian Tsar. By 1914, he was an experienced underground activist, dedicated to creating the basis of a future Polish national army. He aligned his forces with the Central Powers but concentrated only on fighting Russia and did not enjoy or desire the full confidence of his German allies. He ended the war a German prisoner.

In November 1918, Piłsudski was appointed as the effective head of a revived Poland – and given the enormous task of rebuilding a state. He had to do so while simultaneously fighting a war against Bolshevik Russia, successfully repulsing the Russian Red Army at the Battle of Warsaw in 1920. He retired from politics three years later, but returned in 1926 to head a coup that restored him to power as a military strongman, until his death in 1935.

The Rif War

At the beginning of the twentieth century, the mountainous Rif region of northern Morocco was virtually untouched by either Europeans or Arabs, and jealously guarded by the Berber tribespeople who lived there. However, in 1912 the Treaty of Fez had divided Morocco into colonial 'spheres of interest', awarding Spain theoretical control over the Rif. Subsequent Spanish exploitation of mining rights in the region led to violent clashes and by 1920 these had become all-out war.

The leader of Berber resistance was Abd al-Karim, a journalist-turned-guerrilla fighter who inflicted several embarrassing defeats on supposedly stronger Spanish forces, which sparked civil unrest and a military coup back in Spain. The Rif War was ultimately lost when al-Karim overreached himself and invaded French Morocco. In response, France sent more than 150,000 troops to aid the Spanish and al-Karim was exiled to Réunion in the Indian Ocean for the next two decades. Meanwhile, the Rif War marked an important stage in the military career of Colonel Francisco Franco, future fascist dictator of Spain, who was promoted to brigadier general in 1926 in recognition of his role in ending the revolt.

Russian Famine

In Russia, the years 1919–22 cost more lives than the First World War. Following the Bolshevik Revolution of 1917, an alliance of conservative counter-revolutionary forces with international backing, collectively known as the White Army, attacked Bolshevik-controlled western Russia from all directions. At the same time, nationalists in territories previously part of the greater Russian Empire tried to seize independence. Fighting was fierce, and the Bolsheviks imposed a policy of 'war communism', by which they forcibly requisitioned vast quantities of grain and foodstuffs from peasants in the countryside.

The effects were catastrophic. Between the Volga and Ural rivers, an appalling famine set in, peaking between 1921 and 1922. These children were photographed during those crisis years in a refugee camp near Samara. As food vanished, food prices rocketed, black markets sprang up and reports of cannibalism were rife. The famine was an international scandal, and relief efforts were sent from Sweden, the United States, Britain and elsewhere. Yet still, an estimated five million people starved to death or succumbed to famine-related disease.

The Sack of Smyrna

These British citizens posing on the Plymouth dockside in early October 1922 had recently abandoned their homes and possessions as they fled the Turkish city of Smyrna. But they were much more fortunate than the thousands of ethnic Greeks and Armenians who had perished during the sacking of cultured, cosmopolitan Smyrna (Izmir) on the Turkish Aegean coast – the culminating atrocity of the Greco-Turkish War of 1919–22.

This war, like many others, sprang from the ashes of the First World War. In 1920, the Treaty of Sèvres had dismembered the Ottoman Empire. Yet even as this was being negotiated, Greek troops had occupied Smyrna and were trying to conquer further territory, while Turkish nationalists who rejected Sèvres were arming and organizing. As the Greeks were forced back, they exacted brutal vengeance on Turkish Muslim civilians; as Turkish forces advanced, they slaughtered Greeks, Armenians and other minorities. When Turkish troops arrived at Smyrna in September, the city burned.

Atatürk

Mustafa Kemal 'Atatürk' made his name as a military officer while commanding the Ottoman Fifth Army's 19th Division during the battle for Gallipoli in 1915. He subsequently fought in the Caucasus and Palestine, and led the Turkish National Movement during the Greco-Turkish War.

After the Greeks had been defeated, on 29 October 1923 the Republic of Turkey was formed: a single-party state with Kemal as its president. During the next ten years Turkey was reformed and refounded as a modern, secular state. Kemal's reforms jettisoned the roles of sultan and caliph, Ottoman laws, the centrality of Islam, Arabic script, the fez and women's veils. In their place came Western dress, the Latin alphabet, a new calendar and women's suffrage. The Turkish language and Turkish naming conventions were imposed on all citizens. In 1934 Kemal was officially granted the title of 'Atatürk', meaning 'Father of the Turks'. He was mourned both in Turkey and across the world when he died, aged fifty-seven, on 10 November 1938.

The March on Rome

Italy's would-be reformer during the 1920s was Benito Mussolini, a blacksmith's son turned agitator-journalist. In his youth Mussolini was a socialist, but after the First World War he helped establish the *Fasci Italiani di Combattimento* ('Combat Groups') – nationalist vigilantes committed to a cocktail of militaristic, imperialist, racist and reactionary ideas. In 1921 he created the National Fascist Party as a political vehicle for these beliefs.

Post-war Italy was riven with dissatisfaction. Strikes, political violence and revolts against landowners were all underway, while popular sentiment held that Italy had been let down by the Allies in the post-war peace treaties. Conditions were perfect for Mussolini's Fascist movement to flourish. On 27–28 October 1922, Mussolini rallied around 25,000 Fascist supporters – some are seen here in their signature 'blackshirt' uniforms – for a march on Rome. Fearing civil unrest, King Victor Emanuel III immediately appointed Mussolini to lead a coalition government. By 1925, Italian party politics was over, and Mussolini was dictator. He ruled Italy for the next two decades, providing an inspiration to other dangerous European strongmen.

The Ruhr Crisis

In January 1923, the first major crisis in the post-war settlement with Germany unfolded in the Ruhr Valley, a heavily industrialized region of western Germany. At the root of the crisis lay the punitive war reparations imposed on Germany under the terms of the Versailles treaty, which were owed largely to France. By 1922, Germany's new Weimar government had begun to default on this huge war debt. In January 1923, the French prime minister, Raymond Poincaré, sent soldiers to occupy the Ruhr: this photograph shows French troops disarming German police after they marched in. Belgium also sent in soldiers.

Poincaré's assertiveness set France at odds with her British and US allies, but there was little they could do, since it was perfectly legal under the terms of Versailles. More than a hundred German workers were killed during strikes and 'passive resistance' movements, while the crisis also aggravated hyperinflation, which pushed the price of a loaf of bread in Germany to around 200 billion marks.

Adolf Hitler

Resentment at Germany's treatment at Versailles was festering in German society well before the Ruhr crisis. The nation had been humiliated, the economy was broken and many believed the myth that Germany was not defeated in the First World War, but had been betrayed by a cabal of subversives, traitors, Marxists, Jews and 'cultural Bolsheviks'. From these putrid conditions sprang the career of Adolf Hitler.

Hitler had served in the Bavarian Army during the First World War. After the Armistice he joined, rebranded and eventually led the National Socialist German Workers Party (NSDAP, or Nazis). On 8 November 1923, Hitler attempted a coup in Munich to seize control of Bavaria's state government. The so-called Beer Hall Putsch ended in chaos, and Hitler was sentenced to five years in Landsberg prison, where this photograph was taken. Imprisonment was no hardship. Hitler was allowed many visitors, served only a fraction of his sentence, and dictated the text of his autobiographical manifesto, *Mein Kampf* ('My Struggle'), to fellow inmates. When he was released, he was ready to resume what would become the twentieth century's most notorious political career.

The Great Syrian Revolt

In Syria, the imposition of a French mandate crushed Arab hopes for independent rule. It also created new tensions as, unlike the Ottomans, the French had little sense of the complex local politics. In 1925, the Druze community south of Damascus rose up under the war veteran Sultan al-Atrash and rebelled against French rule, which, said al-Atrash, had 'choked freedom' and 'stolen' Syria. Their uprising soon spread across the region.

The result was the two-year Great Syrian Revolt. This photograph was taken after the Battle of Rashaya (20–24 November 1925), in which a hilltop fortress held by French Foreign Legion cavalrymen was attacked by a larger force of Druze fighters, and vicious close-quarter combat took place around the perimeter walls. The Great Syrian Revolt was eventually defeated by superior French military technology and numbers, while al-Atrash fled into exile in Transjordan and thousands of his people were left dead or destitute. The French mandate in Syria lasted until the end of the Second World War.

Palestine

As Hitler began his rise, his eventual nemesis, Winston Churchill, was serving as colonial secretary in the British government. In this photograph, taken on 28 March 1921, Churchill is attending a tree-planting ceremony to mark the site for a new Hebrew University at Mount Scopus, Jerusalem.

After 1918, the Ottoman Near East had been carved up into British and French 'mandates', along lines laid out in the secret Anglo-French Sykes–Picot Agreement of 1916. Britain's mandates included Palestine, Transjordan and Mesopotamia, which was renamed Iraq.

Churchill was ambivalent about these mandates, worrying that they were economic and political liabilities. He also had to wrestle with the question of Jewish settlement. In 1917, the Balfour Declaration had seemed to promise a Jewish National Home in Palestine. Yet Arab fighters, spurred on by desires for liberation, had helped the British push the Ottomans out of Palestine. Churchill wrote that the immigration 'will be good for the world, good for the Jews, good for the British Empire'. He hoped it would also be 'good for the Arabs… and that they shall not be sufferers or supplanted'. Time would tell.

1930– The Rise of Fascism 1936

On the morning of 14 June 1934, a Junkers Ju52 aeroplane circled over Venice. Adolf Hitler, the chancellor of Germany, did not want to touch down too early, and anyway the brief diversion afforded him his first glimpse of Piazza San Marco and the city's other famous buildings. Accompanying him was his personal photographer, Heinrich Hoffmann, a committed Nazi since 1920 and the man entrusted with cultivating the image of Germany's Führer.

Hitler landed at Venice's airport at noon, exactly on time. The Italian dictator, Benito Mussolini, stood waiting: it was the first time the two men had met, and Mussolini, accompanied by an entourage and an enormous press pack, was dressed in full military uniform. Hitler, perhaps expecting a more discreet visit, was in rumpled civvies and a brown overcoat. He saluted, but Mussolini leaned in to shake Hitler's hand – and the subtle power play was snapped by the press. More handshakes would follow, including one during ceremonies at the Piazza San Marco, where this image (*previous page*) was captured by Hoffmann. In all of them, Hitler appeared something of a supplicant.

Adolf Hitler had been Germany's chancellor for almost eighteen months, but he was still some way from achieving the absolute power he craved. By contrast, Mussolini was approaching a decade as Italy's dictator and was the object of a personality cult he enthusiastically encouraged. At Venice, therefore, Mussolini was the senior statesman, whose tactics Hitler had studied, and whose blessing Hitler had sought.

Hitler stayed two days in Italy and it did not take long for relations with his host to sour. With the exception of his service in the First World War, this was Hitler's first ever trip outside Germany or Austria. But he was unimpressed by Italian military displays, and the two leaders had a blazing row about Austria. Hitler made plain that he expected Austria eventually to be absorbed into the German Reich; Mussolini insisted on Austrian independence, which Italy was guaranteeing with troops. Yet despite this awkward encounter, the fortunes of Mussolini's Fascist Italy and Hitler's Nazi Germany would be closely intertwined as the years wore on.

Some of the conditions that allowed these two grandstanding dictators and their totalitarian parties to flourish in the 1930s could be traced back to the terrible legacy of the First World War and the flawed attempts at peacemaking that had followed. Others were unique to the times. Exhausted and understandably gun-shy, Britain and France preferred containment and appeasement to the prospect of a renewed fight with Germany, and many in both those countries reckoned fascism a lesser evil than Russian-style communist revolution. The League of

Nations, established as an international arbiter and peacekeeper, lacked the moral authority and muscle to enforce its own mandate.

Meanwhile, after the Wall Street Crash of 1929, the Great Depression tore a hole in the economy of virtually every Western nation, leaving millions of ordinary voters ruined and susceptible to populist, hateful messages. The German elites who allowed Hitler to become chancellor in January 1933 underestimated their man: it took him less than a month to start destroying Weimar democracy, and when the parliament building burned down in February 1933, Hitler had a ready-made excuse to rule by *diktat*. Two weeks after meeting Mussolini, Hitler made another chilling demonstration of his ruthlessness in the murderous purge called the 'Night of Long Knives'.

For all those who wanted to see, the true course of fascism was hiding in plain sight in the early 1930s. Hitler – long committed to a racist, expansionist vision of Germany's future – had already begun to menace Austria's leaders, who in 1934 adopted their own form of fascism as they struggled to keep their country independent. Meanwhile, Mussolini was using the Italian military to realize his own imperial dreams in North and East Africa.

At the same time, the balance within the relationship between the two dictators was altering. In August 1934, the German president, Paul von Hindenburg, died and Hitler took full power over Germany. And as 1935 closed, Mussolini recognized the growing might of Nazi Germany and the strategic desirability of a closer relationship. Henceforth, there was no doubt about which of the two dictators was pre-eminent.

The Great Depression

At the end of October 1929, the US stock market crashed. Across several days' trading, between 'Black Thursday' (24 October) and 'Black Tuesday' (29 October), the value of American stocks dropped by around 25 per cent, wiping billions of dollars off the market and sparking the worst global financial crisis in history. In the weeks that followed, economies across the world collapsed into a spiralling recession – the Great Depression – which lasted for more than a decade and produced the conditions for another general war.

In the United States the recession was particularly severe, with around one in four workers unemployed. The misery brought about by this economic crisis created a surge in popularity for political parties on the extremes. Membership of the US Communist Party increased to at least 65,000 during the 1930s. Activists like these, photographed in San Francisco, found willing audiences as they protested against evictions of farmers, and demanded unemployment relief, along with the guarantee of trade union, labour and civil rights.

FDR

On 5 July 1932 Franklin Delano Roosevelt – or FDR – was photographed in the office he kept as governor of New York State. Days earlier in Chicago, on being nominated as the Democratic candidate for the presidency of the United States, FDR had boldly promised a 'New Deal'. This signature policy would forever be associated with the presidency he assumed in 1933 and relinquished only when he died in office during his fourth term, in 1945.

Roosevelt was a bona-fide American aristocrat, an alumnus of Harvard University and Columbia Law School and an accomplished, experienced politician. He was physically tough: after contracting polio in the early 1920s he relied on leg braces, a cane and a protective press to hold him upright. This disability did not stop him from taking on one of the most daunting tasks to face any American president: saving America from the destruction wrought by the Great Depression. Roosevelt's New Deal was a bracingly un-American scheme of massive federal intervention and economic stimulus. His critics called it socialism, communism and worse – but FDR dragged the USA through the 1930s and left a lasting legacy to American politics.

Manchukuo

The League of Nations had been established after the First World War with the aim of preventing and settling conflicts. Few incidents better suggested the League's basic weakness than its failure to prevent a Japanese invasion of Manchuria, in north-east China.

Manchuria was a tempting target for Japan, since it was rich in natural resources and offered a possible bulwark against advances by Soviet Russia. On 18 September 1931, Japanese troops invaded, and this photograph was taken a day later. China appealed to the League of Nations for help but this did little good. Japanese forces remained in Manchuria and the province was renamed 'Manchukuo'. In October 1932 the League of Nations eventually declared the puppet state illegal and demanded Japanese withdrawal. In response, Japanese delegates walked out of the League. Japan remained in possession of Manchuria, emboldened even if diplomatically isolated. This territorial grab has even been described as the first conflict of the Second World War.

The Chaco War

As the Depression spiralled out from the United States, in Latin America a savage war broke out between Bolivia and Paraguay, known as the Chaco War. The Chaco region was especially valuable because it gave landlocked Bolivia and Paraguay access to the Atlantic Ocean, and because oil had been discovered in the foothills of the Andes.

In 1932, periodic skirmishes between the two countries erupted into all-out warfare. To begin with, patriotic Bolivian reservists, like those photographed here, flocked to be mobilized. But within a year, mass conscription and a series of defeats had begun to sap morale. Bolivia began with a larger, German-trained army and a modest air force. However, the draftees, many of them indigenous Amerindians from the highlands, suffered grievously from tropical diseases. Gradually, the Paraguayans gained the upper hand, until, in 1935, an armistice was agreed under pressure from the USA and neighbouring countries. Paraguay won most of the Chaco, while Bolivian access to Atlantic via the River Paraguay was confirmed in a final treaty, signed in 1938. By then, the war had cost 100,000 lives through fighting and disease.

Chancellor Hitler

Against the backdrop of the Great Depression, extremist parties in Germany made huge gains at the ballot box. In 1928 the Nazis held just twelve seats in the Reichstag, yet by 1932 they were the largest party, with 230 seats. The Nazis' paramilitary *Sturmabteilung* (SA), defying banning orders, fought vicious street battles with communist militias, while Hitler and other high-ranking Nazis spread the Nazi message far and wide with rabble-rousing speeches. In 1932 Hitler ran for election as German president. He was defeated by Paul von Hindenburg, but garnered 13 million votes along the way. The Nazi creed of national and economic renewal, strong leadership and aggressive scapegoating of blame groups, including Jews, all found a willing audience.

By early 1933 that audience included Hindenburg himself. The moderate, centrist parties of the Weimar Republic had failed to form a coalition capable of keeping the Nazis out of power, and Hindenburg was eventually persuaded that the Nazis could be 'managed'. On 30 January – a few weeks before this photograph was taken – he formally appointed Hitler as chancellor. It was a fatal miscalculation.

The Reichstag Fire

On the morning of 28 February 1933, barely a month after Hitler became chancellor, Berlin policemen surveyed the ruins of the Reichstag. The previous evening, the parliament building had been set ablaze. A young Dutch communist called Marinus van der Lubbe was arrested, tried and guillotined for setting the fire.

Hitler declared it a communist plot, demanded emergency powers to deal with the crisis and had thousands of political opponents locked up. A snap election on 5 March, conducted amid intimidation by Nazi paramilitaries, delivered the Nazis 50 per cent of the vote and enough seats in parliament to ally with other nationalists and pass the Enabling Act. It allowed Hitler to rule by decree. The Communist Party was banned, a new Ministry of Propaganda controlled the media, and 'undesirables' in the civil administration and judiciary were purged. By May, trade unions were under a Nazi umbrella organization. In July, a law was passed banning new political parties. The reality of a one-party state dawned.

Italian Libya

The absence of decisive global leadership in the 1930s allowed Benito Mussolini's Italian Army to pursue a long-standing colonial project in North Africa. Twenty years previously, Italy had fought a war with the Ottoman Empire to capture the province of Tripolitania (roughly, modern Libya), which they divided into two territories: Italian Tripolitania and Italian Cyrenaica.

As a young man, Mussolini had opposed war in Libya. But by 1930, he was a dictator with dreams of a 'Second Roman Empire', and he authorized General Rodolfo Graziani to move into North Africa to put down a stubborn anti-Italian rebellion. Graziani carried out his orders with extreme prejudice, incarcerating Cyrenaica's population in concentration camps and mounting air attacks. At least 40 per cent of Cyrenaica's inhabitants died.

By 1932 the so-called Pacification of Libya was complete. Cyrenaica and Tripolitania were combined and Libyans were inducted into the Fascist Party and the Italian Army. Whether the Libyan boy shown here raising his arm in a Fascist salute was mimicking his elders in jest or seriousness is not clear. Whatever the case, it was plain that by the early 1930s, fascism was on the march.

Persecuting the Jews

Hitler's rambling memoir-manifesto, *Mein Kampf*, had made little secret of his dislike for Jewish people, whom he described variously as maggots, vipers and parasites. He evoked a vicious and broad-based European tendency to anti-Semitism that stretched back to the Middle Ages, and updated it for the 1930s by suggesting that Jews were to be identified with both greedy capitalists and Marxist revolutionaries.

On taking power, the Nazis turned this cocktail of bigotry and hate into government policy. In 1933 Jews were removed from the German Civil Service, and subsequently banned from other public services and professions, including teaching and medicine. This graffiti, daubed on a shop window in that year, reads: 'Germans!!! Don't buy from Jews.' And this was only the start. In September 1935 the Nuremberg Laws were enacted and Jews were denied German citizenship. Many began to leave Germany. Those who stayed were pushed to the margins of society. It would not be long before the mass murders began.

RAEL

ht beim

uden

Austrofascism

With Nazi Germany to the north and Mussolini's Italy to the south, it was perhaps unsurprising that in the 1930s Austria moved decisively towards authoritarianism. In March 1933 the Austrian chancellor, Engelbert Dollfuss, a pugnacious politician who stood less than five feet tall, took advantage of a political crisis to suspend parliament and rule by decree. Political parties including the Communists and Austrian Nazis were outlawed, and a clampdown on civil liberties took place. In early 1934 Dollfuss's dictatorial rule provoked open warfare between government forces and leftist paramilitaries. This photograph was taken in Vienna on 12 or 13 February, at a housing development known as the Goethehof.

Although a fascist, Dollfuss was not a Nazi, and he strongly rejected arguments for a unification of Germany and Austria. He earned his reward on 25 July 1934, when a group of Austrian Nazis burst into his office and murdered him. Dollfuss was succeeded by Kurt Schuschnigg, who tried to resist the Nazification of the state. Ultimately, he also failed. Within four years Germany had annexed Austria into Hitler's Third Reich.

The Night of the Long Knives

Much of the Nazis' success in Germany was rooted in the violence of the SA, led from 1931 by Ernst Röhm – pictured here in his office, in front of an eighteenth-century Flemish tapestry. Under Röhm, the SA grew its numbers and ambition: by 1934 there were more than three million members, many of whom agitated for a 'second revolution' of an overtly anti-capitalist nature. Yet at the same time the SA was becoming redundant to the Nazi cause: now that Hitler was chancellor, he controlled the entire machinery of the German state, including the police and armed forces.

Between 30 June and 2 July 1934, Hitler moved against the troublesome SA and various other political enemies. The smaller elite Nazi paramilitary, the SS (*Schutzstaffel*), arrested and killed around 200 SA officers, dissident Nazis and former opponents, citing evidence of a plot by Röhm to seize power. Röhm refused to commit suicide, so was shot in a prison cell. The 'Night of the Long Knives' was brutal, efficient and a chilling illustration of Hitler's utter ruthlessness in consolidating his power.

Oswald Mosley

Fascism was not limited to continental Europe. In the 1930s, the blackshirts of the British Union of Fascists (BUF) brought their own brand of thuggish nationalism to the streets of London. Their leader was Sir Oswald Mosley, pictured here (*second from the left*) in 1935. Elected as a Member of Parliament aged just twenty-two, Mosley was an archetypal establishment figure. He was a brilliant orator but a permanently restless figure, sitting as a Conservative, Independent and Labour MP before founding the New Party in 1931, but losing his seat as a result.

In the early 1930s Mosley travelled to Mussolini's Italy, then returned and rebranded his party as the BUF, complete with paramilitary-style uniform, anti-Semitic rhetoric and populist agitation. Fights and ugly protests accompanied BUF rallies and marches, culminating in October 1936 in the Battle of Cable Street, a clash between BUF members, anti-fascists and police in east London. After Cable Street, some in the BUF split to form the overtly Nazi National Socialist League. Mosley himself was interned in 1940, along with hundreds of other suspected fifth columnists. After the war, he moved to Paris, where he died in 1980.

The Nuremberg Rallies

Overblown, military-style, quasi-religious rallies were a regular feature of Nazi propaganda, with a history dating back to the 1920s. During the 1930s Nazi rallies became annual fixtures, invariably held in the Bavarian city of Nuremberg and themed around the Nazis' supposed values, including 'Honour', 'Victory' 'Power' and (rather ironically) 'Freedom'.

The participants photographed here are members of the *Reicharbeitsdienst* (RAD) – a national voluntary labour service. The military attire and training of the RAD spoke to both the general Nazi obsession with uniforms and discipline and to the means by which Hitler had already begun to circumvent the restrictions of Versailles. The treaty limited the German Army to a strength of 100,000 volunteer troops; the RAD did not count towards that quota.

From 1933 onwards, Nuremberg rallies tended to celebrate major milestones in the Nazi accrual of power. The rally that year marked Hitler's appointment as chancellor. The 1936 rally trumpeted German remilitarization of the Rhineland. It was not difficult to see which way the Nazis, and the country they now controlled, were heading.

Leni Riefenstahl

Nazi Party rallies were major propaganda events, and as such were memorialized for posterity by some of the most talented visual artists in the Third Reich. The most famous documentarian of Nazi festivities was the film director Leni Riefenstahl. Riefenstahl had been a popular actress in the German genre of alpine-themed films (*Bergfilme*). Her film about the 1934 Nuremberg Rally, *Triumph of the Will*, consolidated her directorial reputation. It was seen across Germany and admired across the world for its superlative cinematic technique, despite its lamentable subject matter.

This photograph of Riefenstahl was taken on 12 July 1936 when she was working on a film to document the Berlin Olympic Games. Next to her (*centre*) is Carl Diem, the chief organizer of the Games. The film Riefenstahl eventually produced, *Olympia*, is still considered a ground-breaking sports documentary. Riefenstahl survived the Second World War and worked until her death in 2003, at the age of 101. She consistently denied having ever been a committed Nazi, but questions about her relationship with Hitler and her knowledge of the Holocaust dogged her all her life.

The Abyssinia Crisis

As the Nazis gathered strength, in
Italy Benito Mussolini remained
determined to expand his territories
in Africa, setting his sights on the
empire of Abyssinia (Ethiopia). In
early December 1934, troops from
the colony of Italian Somaliland
skirmished with Abyssinian forces at
the Walwal oasis. The Abyssinian
emperor, Haile Selassie, complained
to the League of Nations but it did
him no good. On 3 October 1935,
Mussolini's invasion began. Italian
troops, around 100,000-strong, were
heavily outnumbered, but they had
air support, machine guns, artillery
and mustard gas, while many of
Selassie's forces still wielded spears
and nineteenth-century rifles.

Belatedly, the League of Nations
tried to impose economic sanctions on
Italy. Mussolini ignored the sanctions,
secured Hitler's backing for his war,
withdrew Italy from the League of
Nations, and made private pacts with
Britain and France assuring him that
there would be no serious punishment.
The Abyssinian capital, Addis Ababa,
fell in May 1936 and Haile Selassie fled
into exile. The international community
was shown to be unable or unwilling
to intervene against fascist aggression.

Darkness Falling

I n 1938 the American photographer Margaret Bourke-White, working for *Life* magazine, was *en route* for Czechoslovakia when she arrived in Spain, in the middle of that country's civil war. The simple note scribbled on the back of this photograph only hints at the destruction that war had already caused. It reads: 'Spain – Angeles Gonzalez – 7 years old – refugee from Madrid.'

Like most of Bourke-White's photographs, this one was carefully posed and meticulously constructed – in this case to deliver an emotional message about the nature of the war. It is not reportage. But it does speak to a truth perceived by Bourke-White and the many other artists, writers and activists who were drawn to document the Spanish Civil War. The conflict they interpreted was fought between Spain's Republicans and Nationalists, but it was also a proxy conflict for the greater international struggle that lay ahead – and a premonition of the immense human suffering that was to come. Angeles Gonzalez was just one refugee among thousands.

Since the late 1920s, Spanish trades unions and republicans, along with separatists in Catalonia and the Basque region, had challenged Spain's authoritarian, royalist and Catholic traditions. By 1931, popular dissatisfaction had reached a crisis point: the monarchy fell, and a republic was declared. In 1936, tensions between the dizzying array of factions on the right and left once again boiled over, and on 17 July an attempted military coup ushered in the civil war.

From early on, it was more than a localized struggle. In the context of the unhappy state of European politics, it was seen as a clash of ideologies, which attracted international involvement. Nazi Germany lent the Nationalist coalition (which included the Falange, or Spanish fascists) an air force and troops in the shape of the Condor Legion; Mussolini sent planes and Italian soldiers. By 1937, the Nationalists largely ruled the air, and the violence they were able to deal out from above, including to civilians, shocked the world. On the other side, Spain's Republican coalition was supported either overtly or secretly by the USSR, France and Mexico, and by the 'International Brigades': volunteers who travelled to fight, from Britain, the United States and elsewhere.

The writer George Orwell, who volunteered with a Republican militia, said he was fighting for 'common decency'. But common decency was a losing cause. By the time Margaret Bourke-White moved on to central Europe, hope for a civilized end to this war was rapidly vanishing. Madrid – the Spanish capital and young Angeles Gonzalez's home town – fell to the Nationalists on 28 March 1939. General Francisco Franco declared victory for the

Nationalists four days later. Half a million Spaniards had died, and many more would follow in recriminatory executions.

Outside Spain, fascism and militarism were on the march too. From mid-December 1937 to late January 1938, Japanese forces invaded China, ransacking Shanghai and Nanjing, where barely imaginable atrocities occurred. In April 1939, Mussolini's troops conquered Albania. That same month, Spain joined Germany, Italy and Japan in signing the formal alliance of the world's leading hard-right regimes, known as the 'Anti-Comintern Pact'.

Inevitably, perhaps, it was Adolf Hitler who turned alliance-building into all-out war. At home, the Nazification of Germany proceeded at pace. Increasingly oppressive laws aimed to make life for Jews in Germany so unbearable that they would emigrate; many who did not leave were sent to the Reich's burgeoning concentration camps, where they joined political prisoners, homosexual men and other so-called anti-socials including alcoholics, prostitutes and homeless people.

Abroad, Hitler began the expansion of the Reich of which he had long dreamed. In March 1938 German troops marched into Austria, to absorb the country into the Third Reich. Immediately afterwards, Hitler turned his attention to Czechoslovakia, first bullying the British prime minister, Neville Chamberlain, into allowing him to take the Sudetenland, then in March 1939 sweeping into what was left. In August of the same year, an audacious agreement of neutrality was brokered with the USSR by Hitler's foreign minister, Joachim von Ribbentrop. Its greedy aim was to carve up north-eastern Europe between the two powers.

On 1 September 1939, Nazi Germany invaded Poland. Three days later, the Second World War began in earnest.

Lleida

On 2 November 1937, bombers of the Condor Legion – the air force supplied by Nazi Germany to support the Nationalist faction in the Spanish Civil War – bombed the Catalan town of Lleida in northeastern Spain. Several hundred people were killed. Among them were forty-eight children and their teachers attending class at the Liceu Escolar.

This scene, captured in the aftermath of the bombing, was depressingly familiar across Spain during the civil war that raged from 1936 to 1939. After fighting began, Hitler authorized the deployment of German ground and air troops to the region, along with transport planes, fighters and bombers. Their presence in Spain served two purposes: to distract international attention from German designs on central Europe; and to provide a test bed for military hardware, which would be put to use in the general European war to follow.

Lleida was not the only atrocity committed by the Condor Legion. On 26 April 1937, German and Italian bombers had laid waste to the Basque town of Guernica (Gernika). The carnage was immortalized in Pablo Picasso's painting *Guernica*.

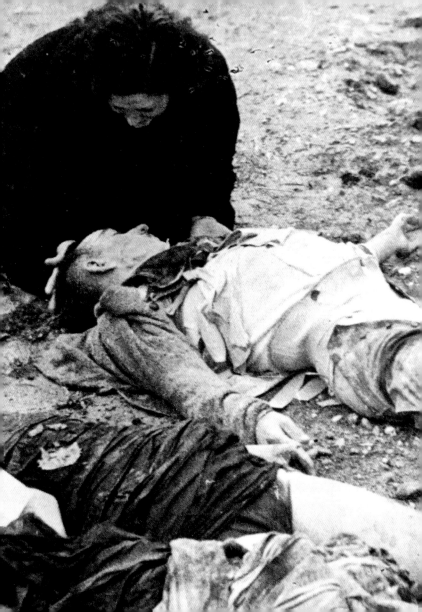

The Battle of Shanghai

On the other side of the world, a major war erupted in 1937 between Japan and China. The Japanese had occupied Manchuria earlier in the decade, establishing the puppet state of Manchukuo; this had been followed by frequent clashes between Chinese and Japanese troops, particularly around Mongolia.

A fragile truce was broken dramatically on 7 July 1937, near Beijing. Within five weeks, the Imperial Japanese Army and Navy had invaded China and descended on the coastal city of Shanghai. The battle for the city lasted for three months and sucked in approximately one million men. The Japanese attacked with infantry, amphibious landings, artillery barrages, naval bombardment and airborne bombing raids; this photograph was taken on 22 August, and shows Japanese defenders tugging a conquered tank into their lines.

After a ferocious and often desperate Chinese defence, Shanghai finally fell at the end of November, and the Japanese marched on the capital of Nanjing. Its fate was atrocious: a six-week orgy of killing, sexual violence and looting known to posterity as 'the Rape of Nanjing'.

The Hitler Youth

While Spain and China erupted into violence, in Germany Hitler was growing more confident with every passing month and enjoying the luxuries that came with the position of supreme leader. This photograph was taken at his private holiday retreat in the Obersalzberg: the Berghof, a luxurious chalet in the Bavarian Alps. Leading Nazis and businessmen, generals, foreign leaders and royalty were welcomed there, along with artists and musicians. The visitors pictured here are members of the Hitler Youth (*Hitlerjugend*), a Nazified perversion of the Boy Scouts, which indoctrinated young men into the tenets of National Socialism and the Führer cult.

The Hitler Youth was just one way in which young Germans were trained in Nazi orthodoxy. The movement existed in parallel with a schooling system that emphasized a Nazi version of history, racial purity and physical education. Meanwhile, the League of German Girls prepared girls for the traditionalist roles of housekeeping and child-rearing that suited Nazi ideology. Brainwashing the young was important because it worked: Hitler Youth fighters numbered among the very last defenders of the Reich in 1945.

The Anti-Comintern Pact

On 25 November 1937 several of Nazi Germany's most important figures visited the Japanese Embassy in Berlin, to celebrate the first anniversary of the Anti-Comintern Pact. Three weeks earlier, Mussolini's Italy had joined the pact; Francisco Franco would commit Spain to the alliance in 1939, and other powers joined in the years to 1941. The Anti-Comintern Pact's members opposed the worldwide spread of communism as fostered by the USSR through the Communist International (Comintern) organization. They also shared ideologically sympathetic, authoritarian governments, aggressive foreign policies and a broad contempt for the League of Nations.

This photograph, taken that evening, includes a number of high-ranking Nazis. Next to the Japanese ambassador, Kintomo Mushakōji (*foreground, centre*), is Adolf Hitler himself. To the right, holding court in satin-striped trousers, is Hermann Göring, head of the Luftwaffe and Hitler's *de facto* deputy. To Hitler's left stands Alfred Rosenberg, an obsessive political and racial theorist, who was influential in concocting key elements of Nazi ideology. He was hanged after the Nuremberg trials, in 1946.

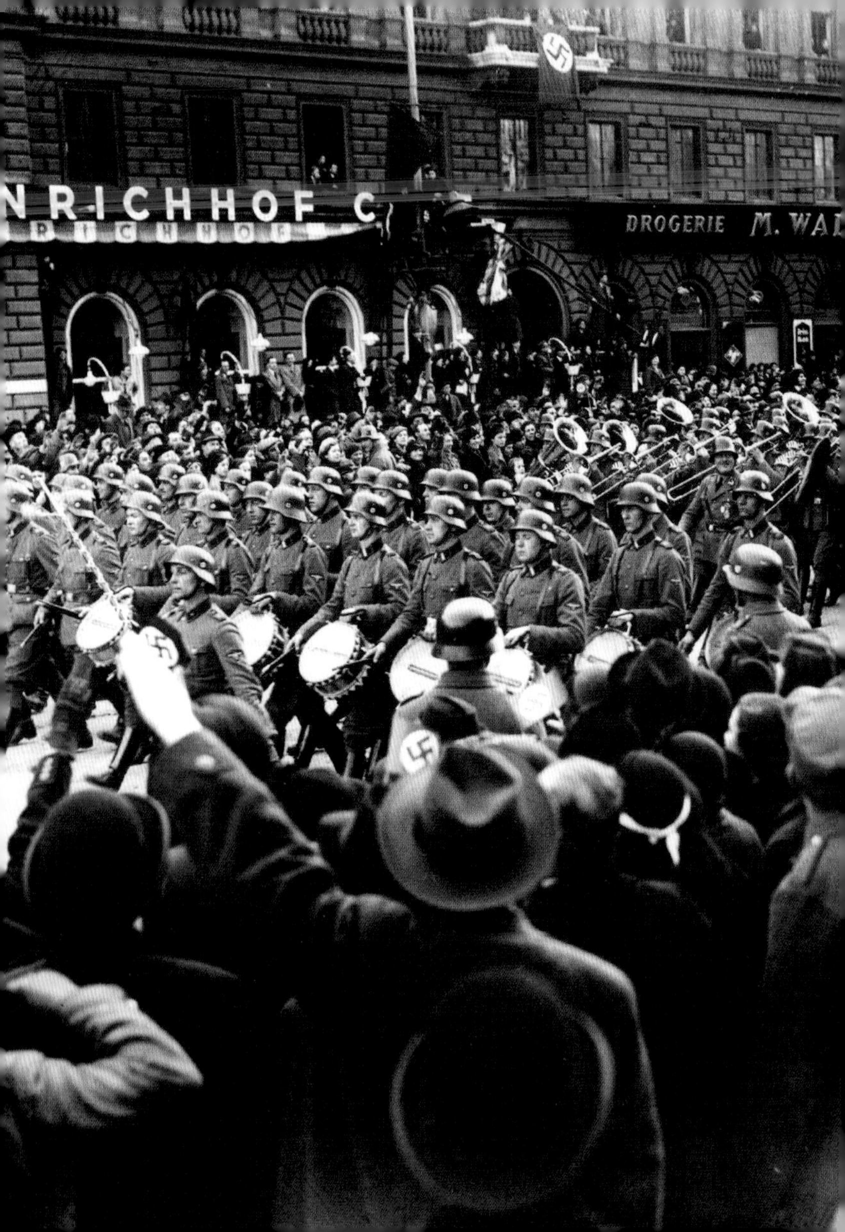
NRICHHOF C
DROGERIE M. WA

Anschluss

Expanding the borders of the German Reich was a major theme of Nazi foreign policy in the 1930s, particularly where it could be argued that this would bring 'ethnic Germans' back into their homeland. This policy was known as *Heim ins Reich* ('Home to the Reich') and it was realized most spectacularly in March 1938, when German soldiers swarmed into Austria to enforce the 'Anschluss': political union between the two nations, with Germany as dominant partner.

Previously, 'Austrofascism' had prized Austrian independence. Yet public opinion now wavered. In February 1938, Hitler summoned Austria's chancellor, Kurt Schuschnigg, to a meeting and delivered an ultimatum: hand powers to the Austrian Nazi Party, or face annexation. Schuschnigg initially agreed, but demanded a public vote. Hitler's patience ran out. On 12 March 1938, a day before Schuschnigg's planned vote, German soldiers marched into Austria. Many of them were greeted with cheers and Nazi salutes. A year later a new plebiscite was held, after which it was announced that more than 99 per cent of Austrian voters had approved the Anschluss.

Appeasement

Prior to the Anschluss, Hitler had defied the terms of Versailles by marching German troops into the supposedly demilitarized Rhineland. Emboldened, Hitler announced his desire to take over a large, German-majority portion of Czechoslovakia, known as the Sudetenland. This amounted to a full-blown crisis for Europe's great powers, and the task of dealing with Hitler effectively fell to the British prime minister, Neville Chamberlain, pictured here in Downing Street, in London.

On 29 September 1938 Chamberlain met Hitler at Munich, along with Mussolini and the French prime minister, Édouard Daladier. There, the leaders agreed that Germany could annexe the Sudetenland. In return, Hitler promised that this would be his last territorial demand. For a brief while, Chamberlain was a hero, invited on to the balcony of Buckingham Palace where he was regaled with rounds of 'For He's a Jolly Good Fellow'. But not everyone was convinced. And in the view of Winston Churchill, the agreement Chamberlain had struck at Munich was 'a total and unmitigated defeat'. He would not have to wait very long to be proven correct.

The Fall of Czechoslovakia

In early October 1938, German troops moved into the Sudetenland and were met by Sudeten Germans like these, photographed on 3 October, who flashed stiff-armed Nazi salutes. At Munich, Hitler had not anticipated such British and French willingness to cut a deal, and had been prepared for the violent conquest of all of Czechoslovakia. Nevertheless, Hitler did not have to wait long for the country to collapse of its own accord.

The Munich Agreement also permitted Poland to annexe the territory known as Zaolzie, while Hungary was awarded part of Slovakia. In March 1939 the rest of Slovakia seceded and became a Nazi puppet state. The Wehrmacht moved swiftly into the Czech heartlands of Bohemia and Moravia to claim what was left. Hitler visited Prague Castle and declared a German Protectorate, and Nazification began in swift and predictable fashion, with the persecution of Jews, a clampdown on press freedom and the introduction of a police state.

Kristallnacht

Vienna was where Adolf Hitler had taught himself to hate Jews. The city had long been a hub of Jewish intellectual and artistic culture – the city of Sigmund Freud, Gustav Mahler and the playwright Arthur Schnitzler. But in the late 1930s the Anschluss gave licence to ancient and ugly strains of anti-Semitism. In this photograph from 1938, boys under the direction of a Nazi Party official are encouraged in racial prejudice, as one of them daubs *Jud* (Jew) on a property now closed up.

The night of 9–10 November 1938 saw violent attacks on Jewish people, properties, shops, schools and synagogues. Nazi propaganda called these assaults a 'spontaneous' out-pouring of patriotic anger following the murder in Paris of a German diplomat by a Jewish assassin on 9 November. In fact, what took place was a general pogrom, encouraged by senior Nazis and abetted by the SA and police agencies, including the Gestapo. Scores of Jews were killed. This orgy of violence later acquired the name Kristallnacht, the 'Night of Broken Glass', in reference to shattered shopfronts and windows that were seen across Nazi-ruled territories.

Concentration camps

The first Nazi concentration camp was built at Dachau, as soon as Hitler took power in 1933. During subsequent years many more camps were built across Germany and in other Nazi-occupied lands. They included Sachsenhausen, about 23 miles (37km) from Berlin, which opened in 1936 and is pictured here.

Sachsenhausen was a combined camp, barracks and execution place, designed to house thousands of inmates in harsh conditions. Some were put to work, some were tortured or subjected to cruel medical experiments, and others were killed as the guards and their commanders saw fit.

Inmates were identified by colour-coded badges. Red badges were used for political prisoners and pink triangles identified homosexual men. Yellow stars marked out Jewish inmates; in the aftermath of Kristallnacht, thousands of Jews were sent to concentration camps. During the Second World War, the mass murder of Jewish people in death camps would be systemized as the Final Solution.

Kindertransport

After Kristallnacht there could be no doubt about the Nazis' intentions towards Jews in the Reich. In 1938–9 alone, around 100,000 Jews left Germany and Austria, seeking refuge and survival in other lands. But finding a new home was by no means easy: many nations were unwilling to accept large numbers of refugees and Germany did not have a monopoly on anti-Semitism.

One exception to this rule was the Kindertransport programme, by which 10,000 unaccompanied Jewish children under the age of seventeen were resettled in Britain between December 1938 and September 1939. One of the first young people who arrived under that programme was Max Unger (photographed here), who landed on 2 December 1938 at Harwich, along with 200 others, many from a Berlin orphanage attacked on Kristallnacht. This photograph was taken at the Dovercourt Bay Camp in Essex, from where children were sent to live with relatives, foster families or in hostels and camps. According to an inspection report carried out at Dovercourt in January 1939, the children there 'seemed wonderfully happy, considering all they had been through'.

The Great Revolt

During the 1930s, around 60,000 German Jews fleeing the Nazi regime arrived in Palestine. After the First World War, the British had been awarded 'mandatory' control of Palestine and soon found themselves juggling two barely compatible sets of demands. On the one hand, Arab nationalists who had helped fight Ottoman rule during the First World War expected the British to favour their rights. Yet at the same time, Jewish immigrants assumed the British would honour the Balfour Declaration of 1917, which promised them a 'national home'. In the late 1930s the result was a major Arab revolt.

The 'Great Revolt' began in April 1936 with an Arab general strike. Eighteen months later, after an official British report proposed the partition of Palestine, protest gave way to armed insurrection. In response, the British imposed quasi-martial law, while the military and security forces brutally suppressed Arab attacks on officials and infrastructure. This photograph, taken in 1939, shows Palestinian prisoners inside a British Army prison camp at Jenin. The revolt cost at least 5,000 Arab, 400 Jewish and 150 British lives before its end in 1939.

Nazi America

On 20 February 1939, some 20,000 American Nazis gathered at Madison Square Garden in New York City to attend the 'Pro-American Rally': a festival of fascism at which the Nazi swastika and the Stars and Stripes were displayed side by side. The date was near the anniversary of George Washington's birthday (22 February 1732), so behind the main stage the organizers raised a huge image of the first US president (whom they called the 'first fascist'), flanked by Nazi insignia.

The rally was arranged by the German American Bund, an organization that sought to recruit Americans of German descent to propagandize on behalf of Hitler's regime. Although the Bund never attracted more than about 25,000 members, and was largely disowned by Hitler's regime, it nevertheless provided a focal point for would-be Nazis across the Atlantic. It had an imitation SA, known as the Order Service, and a Hitler Youth wing. What it never had, though, was mass popular support. The Pro-American Rally mainly served to turn public opinion against the Bund, and its membership rapidly declined with the outbreak of the Second World War.

The Conquest of Albania

As the Nazi Reich expanded, Mussolini sent Italian troops into Albania, which had long been a target for Italian imperialists. Since 1922 Albania had been ruled by Ahmed Zogu, who raised himself from the position of prime minister to royal status as King Zog I. Albania was a proud nation, but it was also poor, underdeveloped and highly dependent on Italy for trade, financial support and military defence. That Mussolini took the trouble to conquer Albania spoke mostly to his need to keep pace with Hitler.

The invasion began on 7 April 1939. By lunchtime, King Zog had crossed into Greece, taking his wife, infant son and a substantial quantity of gold bullion. The following day the Albanian government surrendered and became an Italian protectorate. This photograph, taken in Rome, illustrates the new state of affairs: Italian officers consecrate the flag of an Albanian regiment, on which the Albanian double-headed eagle has been updated with Italian King Victor Emmanuel's crown of Savoy.

The Nazi-Soviet Pact

There were smiles all round in Moscow on 23 August 1939 when the representatives of Nazi Germany and the USSR signed a Non-Aggression Pact. Joseph Stalin – leader of the USSR since Lenin's death in 1924 – beamed for the camera. Flanking him, the Soviet foreign minister Vyacheslav Molotov (*extreme right*) and his German counterpart, Joachim von Ribbentrop (*arms folded*), exuded satisfaction at one of history's most cynical agreements. Hitler loathed communists and Stalin saw fascism as an urgent threat to the USSR's security. Yet in this agreement, also called the Molotov–Ribbentrop Pact, mutual contempt was laid aside for expedient self-interest.

The pact promised military neutrality, laid the basis for a trading relationship and secretly mapped out a carve-up of Poland and the Baltic states, with Finland and part of Romania to be under Soviet sway. The Pact shocked the world. British and French politicians now knew there was no bulwark to Hitler's ambitions in the east. On 24 August, the Deputy Leader of Britain's Labour Party, Arthur Greenwood, told the House of Commons: 'The war clouds are gathering.'

Invasion of Poland

A week and a day after the Molotov–Ribbentrop Pact was signed, on 1 September 1939, Nazi Germany invaded Poland. Hitler had challenged his generals to complete the conquest in just six weeks. The tactics they adopted were known as blitzkrieg ('lightning war'): a ferocious assault of bomber aircraft, tanks, infantry and artillery. On 17 September, in accordance with the secret protocols of the Molotov–Ribbentrop Pact, Stalin's Red Army invaded from the east. By the end of September, Poland was overrun. This photograph was taken on the first day of the Nazi invasion. It shows the view from inside a large German bomber plane, a Heinkel He 111. The Luftwaffe airman, lying on a cramped platform in the bomber's glazed nose, has a panoramic view of the land below.

Hitler knew very well that Britain and France had sworn to intervene to protect Poland. On 3 September both countries declared war on Germany. This date marked the start of a great-power conflict that had been inevitable, perhaps, since Hitler came to power in 1933. The Second World War had begun.

The Storm of War

I n late May 1940, around 400,000 troops – almost all of them British and French – fell back to the beaches around the port of Dunkirk, in north-east France. Around them, the might of the Nazi war machine was closing in, and the new British prime minister, Winston Churchill, was briefed to expect the rescue of just 10 per cent of the British Expeditionary Force (BEF) trapped there.

He – and they – needed a miracle. Against all the odds, they got one, and it was called Operation Dynamo. Over the course of little more than a week, between 26 May and 4 June 1940, a hastily assembled fleet of Royal Navy ships, aided by a ragtag flotilla of merchant and private vessels (the 'little ships'), raced across the Channel to rescue the soldiers pinned down at Dunkirk. The men on the beaches and those crewing the boats and ships had to endure bombs and strafing by Luftwaffe aircraft, despite valiant sorties flown by Royal Air Force (RAF) pilots to draw them away. Fires raged in the town of Dunkirk. The weather was grim. Long, loud, wet, tense, bloody days spent waiting for salvation drove some men to the verge of madness – and others over it. Yet by the time Operation Dynamo was over, 338,226 Allied soldiers had been saved, two-thirds of them British. It was more than anyone had dared to dream.

On the last day of Operation Dynamo, Churchill told the House of Commons: 'I feared it would be my hard lot to announce the greatest military disaster in our long history.' And indeed, Churchill continued, Dunkirk did represent a catastrophe, with huge loss of life and equipment. Yet the prime minister also offered defiance, to 'outlive the menace of tyranny, if necessary for years, if necessary alone'. 'We shall fight on the beaches,' he promised, 'we shall fight on the landing grounds, we shall fight in the fields and in the streets, we shall fight in the hills; we shall never surrender.'

Operation Dynamo was the largest of several evacuations from French ports in May–June 1940. The corporal photographed here, being helped up a gangplank, is a member of the Auxiliary Military Pioneer Corps – a reservist corps of British light engineers who were involved in most of them during those hair-raising weeks. This chaotic scattering from the shores of France took place because, that spring, Hitler's forces had cut a swathe through western Europe, rudely interrupting the so-called 'Phoney War' that had followed the invasion of Poland. In April, the Nazis launched a lightning invasion of Denmark and Norway. Then, on 10 May 1940, the German Army invaded France, Belgium, Luxembourg and the Netherlands. They skirted the Maginot Line – a vast chain of fortresses and weapons posts designed to protect France from German aggression – and with all the usual speed and relentlessness of blitzkrieg, started an advance towards the coast, encircling as they went the hundreds of thousands of troops of the BEF and French armies who would subsequently be evacuated from Dunkirk.

For the British, further nation-defining tests were imminent. In the Battle of Britain, from July until October 1940, Hermann Göring's Luftwaffe attempted to seize control of Britain's skies so that Operation Sea Lion – a Nazi amphibious invasion across the Channel – could begin. But when the RAF withstood the onslaught, the Battle of Britain bled into the Blitz: a night-bombing campaign against civilian and industrial targets in London and other British cities, which lasted until May 1941.

As Britain resisted, others buckled. Belgium and the Netherlands were occupied. Paris fell on 14 June, and France was divided into a Nazi-occupied zone and a compliant puppet state. Italy entered the war and threatened British interests in Egypt, Palestine and British Somaliland. Elsewhere, the Soviet Union's Winter War delivered victory against Finland in March 1940, while Japan's war with China ground on into a third year. After France's surrender to Germany, the Japanese also began to push into French Indochina.

In the last months of 1940, the relationship between Germany, Italy and Japan – the Axis Powers – was cemented in the Tripartite Pact. From this point onwards, the enemy of one was the enemy of all. The world's conflicts had coalesced into a single world war.

The Battle of the Atlantic

Although the Phoney War of winter 1939–40 saw little fighting on land, it was a different story at sea. When war was declared, Britain and France imposed a naval blockade on Nazi Germany. Hitler retaliated with a counter-blockade. For the next five and a half years, the Atlantic Ocean was a battlefield. During the course of the Second World War, more than 3,000 merchant ships were sunk. Unsurprisingly, anticipating U-boats strikes in the Atlantic was a major goal of British efforts to break the military ciphers used by the Nazis' Enigma machines.

The sailors photographed here were involved in one of the first major naval clashes of the war: the Battle of the River Plate. On 13 December 1939 they were aboard HMS *Exeter* when she, along with HMS *Ajax* and *Achilles*, attacked the German 'pocket battleship' *Admiral Graf Spee* off the coast of Uruguay. Exeter was badly damaged, while *Admiral Graf Spee* was later scuttled on her captain's orders. These sailors are celebrating their safe arrival back in Plymouth.

The Winter War

There was no Phoney War in the east, where in November 1939 Soviet troops invaded Finland. This land grab had been agreed under the secret protocols of the Molotov–Ribbentrop Pact, but it resulted in the USSR's expulsion from the League of Nations. Stalin's generals poured nearly half a million men into the effort and bombarded Finnish cities with incendiary cluster bombs nicknamed 'Molotov bread baskets' by the Finns, after the hated Soviet foreign minister, Vyacheslav Molotov.

While the Soviets possessed impressive firepower and manpower, the Finns fought fiercely and were protected by their climate. Fighters like these Finnish ski troops were more familiar with, and better equipped for, frozen terrain and temperatures that dipped below -40°C. The Soviet Red Army suffered terrible losses: tens of thousands of men were incapacitated by frostbite. Eventually, Soviet numbers won out, and Finland ceded a large amount of territory in the Treaty of Moscow of March 1940. But Stalin's struggle to conquer an apparently feeble neighbour was noted in Germany. This would have profound consequences later.

The Invasion of Norway

Operation Weserübung was the code name for the Nazi invasion of Denmark and Norway, launched on 9 April 1940. Denmark capitulated easily; more dramatic was Norway's battle.

Controlling the Norwegian coastline would allow German ships and U-boats to threaten Allied merchant convoys in the northern Atlantic. Realizing this, Britain's naval chief, Winston Churchill, had convinced his colleagues to approve mine-laying in Norwegian waters. But before his operation could make significant progress, Hitler ordered an invasion. This photograph was taken a week after the campaign began, and it shows two German soldiers – one a platoon commander – in the snowy landscape north of Oslo.

Allied forces rushed to help the Norwegians resist, but the task of containing the Nazi war machine proved beyond them, and on 7 June the Allies withdrew. The Norwegian king, Haakon VII, was evacuated, along with his family, key government ministers and the country's gold reserves.

The Battle of France

Allied forces were in no position to defend Norway in June 1940 because by that point Hitler's armies were also racing across western Europe. In France, a huge network of concrete forts, pillboxes and artillery positions known as the Maginot Line had been built during the 1930s to oppose any land invasion by German troops. This line was extended in the north by the Ardennes, a wooded and hilly region of Belgium and Luxembourg, held to be impassable.

On 10 May 1940, however, Germany launched a westward attack against Belgium, the Netherlands, Luxembourg and France. Wehrmacht armoured divisions defied Allied expectations by powering directly through the Ardennes. They were led by General Heinz Guderian, a visionary military planner, pictured here in his command vehicle. The speed and focus of the German attack resulted in spectacular gains, achieved within a matter of days. The Netherlands surrendered on 14 May, followed two weeks later by Belgium. By 27 May the British were evacuating the continent. Barely two months after Hitler's invasion of the west began, the Führer was preparing to enter Paris. There seemed to be no limit to his appetites.

Blitzkreig

Nazi blitzkrieg against Belgium and
the Netherlands showed just what a
dangerous military machine Hitler
had assembled during the 1930s.
The campaign began with Luftwaffe
bombing raids on airfields and an
assault by paratroopers in gliders on the
imposing Belgian fort of Eben-Emael.
On 14 May bombing sorties against
the Dutch city of Rotterdam flattened
that city's famous historic centre.
Incendiary attacks set uncontrollable
fires, which burned for days, killing
hundreds and leaving nearly 100,000
Dutch civilians homeless.

Overwhelmed civil defence workers
and emergency services, like these men,
photographed in Brussels at around the
same time, struggled against the flames.
Hard-pressed to resist this furious
assault, Brussels fell to the Nazis on
18 May, and Belgian political unity
disintegrated soon afterwards. On
28 May the Belgian king, Leopold III,
surrendered both his armies and himself
into German hands. This placed the
retreating Allied forces under even
greater pressure and earned Leopold
lasting opprobrium in Belgium and
beyond. The king was placed under
house arrest and would remain a
prisoner for the duration of the war.

Prime Minister Churchill

On the same day that Germany invaded Belgium and the Netherlands – 10 May 1940 – Winston Churchill became prime minister of the United Kingdom. He replaced Neville Chamberlain, who resigned the post after the Allies had failed to protect Norway from Nazi occupation.

Churchill was now sixty-five years old, but he took to his task with the energy of a man half his age. His elevated sense of self and 'bulldog' spirit would prove invaluable to British morale, and his timeless rhetoric provided a soaring, heroic commentary on the Allied war effort. Churchill had been dismissed as a warmonger during the 1930s, when he lambasted those who wished to appease Hitler. Now, as he formed his new War Cabinet, he gave a speech that set the tone. 'I have nothing to offer,' he told MPs, 'but blood, toil, tears and sweat.' Britain's only policy, he said, would be 'to wage war, by sea, land and air, with all our might… against a monstrous tyranny, never surpassed in the dark, lamentable catalogue of human crime.'

The Führer in Paris

Two million Parisians had fled their city before Hitler arrived on 23 June 1940. The previous day French surrender had been confirmed and formalized in the same train carriage that had witnessed the Armistice of November 1918. Having humiliated the French, Hitler had no wish to raze Paris, although he demolished two statues he deemed anti-German, including one of Edith Cavell. In a motorcade of Mercedes cars, he visited the Opéra, before taking in sites from the Arc de Triomphe to Napoleon's tomb at Les Invalides, and Montmartre. His chosen companions on this sightseeing expedition were two architects, Albert Speer (*left*) and Hermann Giesler, along with the sculptor Arno Breker (*right*). Hitler had grand plans for remodelling Berlin and other German cities, so that they might one day outshine Paris.

Although Hitler's visit to Paris lasted a mere three hours and he never returned, he called it the realization of a dream. But for many in France, Nazi occupation would prove to be not so much a dream as a sustained nightmare.

Vichy France

Marshal Philippe Pétain was eighty-four years old when he was recalled to France to serve in the Cabinet in May 1940. As the commander credited with saving Verdun in 1916, Pétain was a national hero. His experience in the Second World War would be very different.

On 16 June, Pétain replaced Paul Reynaud as prime minister and was burdened with agreeing the armistice that confirmed German victory in the Battle of France. The armistice created a German-occupied zone in the north and west of France and allowed a semi-vassal French state to remain in the south, headquartered in Vichy. Pétain became both head of state and premier of this new État Français. An extraordinary personality cult developed around the Marshal, and in 1940–41 he made a tour of Vichy France. Here he is photographed greeting students and receiving bouquets of flowers in Vichy itself.

The Vichy regime lasted until the Allied liberation of France in 1944, after which many of its leading members were condemned as collaborators.

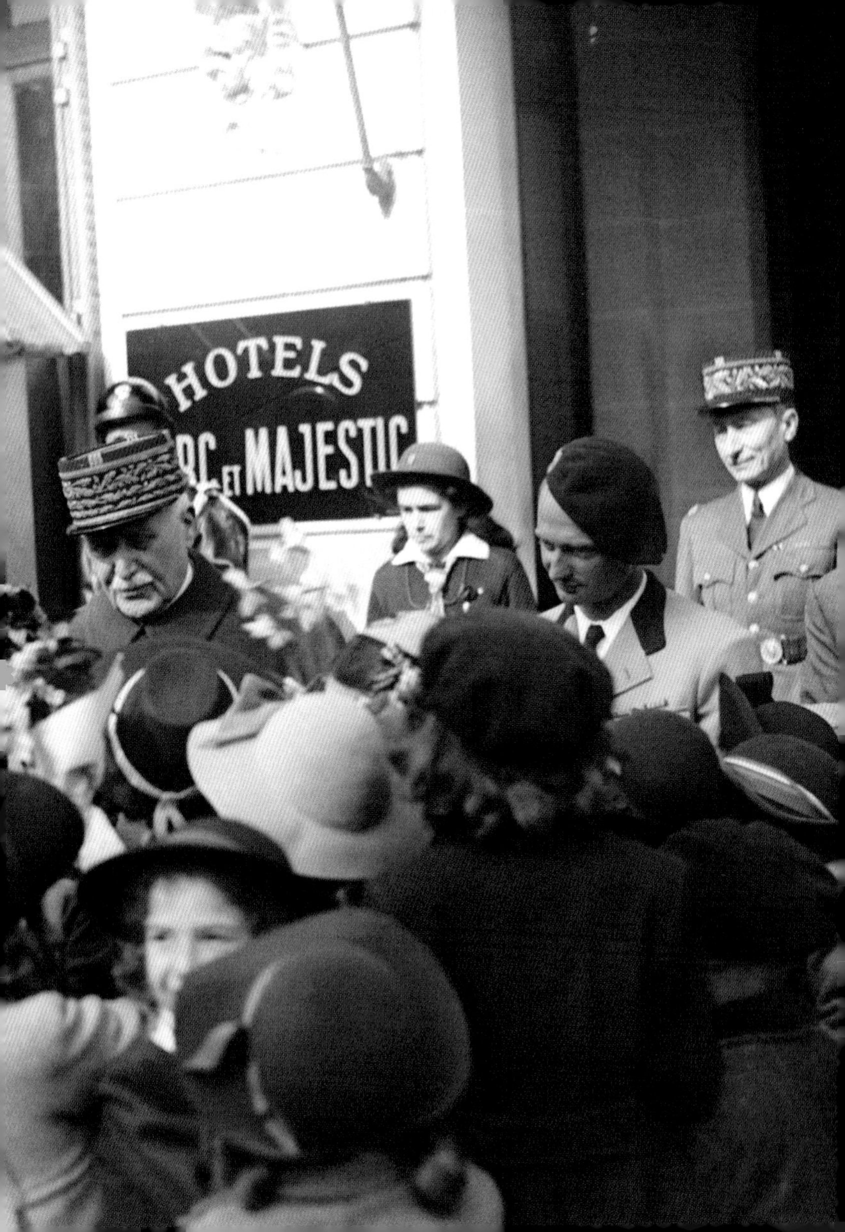
HOTELS
MAJESTIC

The Battle of Britain

Churchill predicted that the fall of France would be followed by the Battle of Britain. He was right. From July to October 1940, the Luftwaffe attacked. Its commander, Hermann Göring, sent waves of German bombers against British targets, while brave but often frighteningly undertrained RAF pilots scrambled to defend the skies. Besides native Britons, the air crews who served in the Battle of Britain included Irishmen, Poles, Czechs, French, Belgians and even volunteer Americans, as well as pilots from the Dominions. Many flew the Supermarine Spitfire, but even more flew the Hawker Hurricane, photographed here by B. J. H. Daventry, a press photographer who served in the RAF.

By October it was clear that the RAF had not been battered into submission, and Hitler was forced to cancel the planned invasion (code-named Operation Sea Lion). For the first time, the Nazis had been halted in their tracks. In another of his great speeches, Churchill said of the RAF: 'Never in the field of human conflict was so much owed by so many to so few.'

Women at War

As soon as the Second World War
started, Britain's parliament passed the
National Service (Armed Forces) Act.
This required all men aged between
eighteen and forty-one to register to
serve in the military, unless they were
ill, involved in essential industries
or could prove that they were
conscientious objectors. Two years later,
the government extended conscription
to British women as well.

Many women had already volunteered, joining organizations including
the Women's Royal Naval Service
(WRNS) and the Women's Auxiliary
Air Force (WAAF). The women
photographed here are members of
the Auxiliary Territorial Service (ATS),
the largest women's service of the war:
a quarter of a million British women
joined up. This photo was taken in
December 1939, when Norma Quaye
(*centre*) was the only black woman in
the service. In addition to cooking,
driving and operating telephones or
typewriters, ATS women could work at
radar stations, on anti-aircraft batteries
or as engineers. In 1945, the eighteen-
year-old Princess Elizabeth (the future
Elizabeth II) joined the ATS, ending
the war with the rank of Junior
Commander.

The Blitz

After the Battle of Britain came the Blitz. From 7 September 1940 until May 1941 the Luftwaffe changed the focus of their campaign, so that instead of targeting airfields, German bombers began to attack cities and their civilian populations. The aim was to damage infrastructure and industrial capacity and terrorize the British into defeatism.

London was the city hardest hit by the Blitz: at the start of the campaign it was attacked on fifty-seven consecutive nights, often with the loss of hundreds of lives at a time. But the bombs fell far and wide across the country. The dramatic rescue pictured here took place in Southampton, a city that hosted vital port facilities and the main Supermarine factory, where Spitfire fighter planes were manufactured.

This photograph, once thought to depict a London scene, was taken in September 1940. It shows a young man called Albert Robbins struggling to pull a bomb victim free of rubble. Later the same day Robbins witnessed a rescue winch slice a girl's legs from her torso. He was so traumatized that he disappeared from his family for three days.

Evacuation

The Battle of Britain and the Blitz put civilians squarely in harm's way. But even before war broke out, a huge evacuation scheme had been in place, designed to take vulnerable people – young mothers, the elderly or disabled and particularly children – out of major cities for temporary relocation in the countryside. The programme was known as Operation Pied Piper and it moved around 3.5 million people between 1938 and 1944.

The children photographed here were being evacuated for the second time. At the outbreak of war, they had been sent to the Sussex coast. When this picture was taken, on 14 July 1940, they were being moved once more, to the Home Counties. The tags they wear typically detailed their name, home address, school and a code number to help the authorities and adult volunteers. The experience of separation could be traumatic – and memories of being sent abruptly and confusingly away from home lingered with some child evacuees all their lives.

The Invasion of Egypt

While Hitler's forces were attacking mainland Britain from above, another theatre of war had opened in North Africa. Mussolini's Italian forces, based in Libya, were preparing to attack Egypt. For the Allies, defending Egypt was vital; the Suez Canal joined the Mediterranean with the Red Sea, allowing British naval and commercial ships to maintain their global reach and access to crucial oil reserves.

The struggle to keep the Italians out of Egypt was known as the Western Desert Campaign. It began in the autumn of 1940 and continued for more than two and a half years. This Italian flamethrower unit was photographed a few months before the campaign began, near the Libyan–Egyptian border. Serious fighting started on 9 September, when the Italian Tenth Army, under Marshal Rodolfo Graziani, swarmed across the border and built fortified camps near the coastal town of Sidi Barrani. In early December, however, the British launched Operation Compass, and the Western Desert Force chased Graziani back into Libya, taking more than 130,000 prisoners and capturing large numbers of tanks and guns as they did so.

Stalemate in China

China had been riven by conflict since 1937. In this photograph, taken in 1940, Chinese civilians line up to form a local self-defence unit; the flag behind them indicates that this is in the part of China still under the sway of Chiang Kai-shek's Nationalist Republic.

Despite the humiliating and bloody defeats of 1937, which had seen the Imperial Japanese Army seize Beijing and Nanjing, the Chinese did not capitulate. The struggle for the important city of Wuhan was appallingly deadly. In June 1938 Chiang ordered the destruction of a major dyke on the Yellow River, thereby deliberately flooding vast swathes of the lands along the riverbanks. This failed to stop the Japanese advance, but it destroyed thousands of Chinese villages and killed anywhere between 500,000 and 1.5 million people. By 1941 the Japanese occupied large tracts of eastern China, but faced a mounting challenge from Chinese communist forces. A stalemate had developed. However, the war in the Far East was about to shift dramatically, as the United States prepared to enter the Second World War.

Invasion

R alph Morse was twenty-four years old when he boarded the US aircraft carrier *Enterprise* in Hawaii. It was January 1942, and although the Second World War had been raging for more than two years, the United States had been an active belligerent for little more than a month. Morse, then a new staff photographer for *Life* magazine, was one of a whole generation of young Americans heading to lands of which many of them had barely even heard.

By Christmas 1942, Morse was on Guadalcanal, one of the Solomon Islands, among US Marines. Joining them on patrol one day, he encountered something that he knew would make 'a great picture… to show people who want to go to war what war was like'. He sent his film back to the USA, sealed in a condom to keep it watertight. Several weeks later, readers of *Life* opened the magazine's 1 February 1943 issue to encounter seven pages of Morse's pictures, including this full-page image. 'A Japanese soldier's skull is propped up on a burned-out Jap tank by U. S. troops,' read the caption. 'Fire destroyed the rest of the corpse.'

Conflict in the Pacific began on 7 December 1941 with the massive Japanese air strike against the US naval base at Pearl Harbor, Hawaii. In the course of around 90 minutes, more than 2,000 US service personnel were killed and 18 ships sunk or seriously damaged. The aim was to ensure that the USA could not interfere with Japan's planned invasions of American, British and Dutch territories in the Far East. The next day, President Roosevelt declared war on Japan, and four days later the declaration was extended to Germany and Italy.

The USA had not been wholly aloof from the war to that point. There had already been violent confrontations between US ships and German vessels in the Atlantic, while US opposition to Japanese imperialism and to the war in China had prompted Roosevelt to prohibit oil sales to Japan. And in March 1941, he had agreed a policy of 'Lend-Lease' to supply friendly powers with war materials. Five months later, acting as if Britain and the USA were already wartime allies, he and Winston Churchill had issued the 'Atlantic Charter': principles for a post-war order based on global cooperation and liberty. It assumed the defeat of fascism and militarism.

Within two weeks of Pearl Harbor, American 'Flying Tigers' pilots were intercepting Japanese bombers over China. On the domestic front, there were mass internments of Japanese Americans. But the USA could not summon sufficient might in the first few months of 1942 to fully halt the Japanese advance in the Pacific. In February, a Japanese army crushed British resistance in Singapore, in what Churchill later called 'the worst disaster and largest capitulation' in British history.

By fighting not only Japan but also the Axis powers in Europe, Roosevelt had made a huge commitment to the Allies. Yet he could hardly have ignored affairs in the west. In April 1941, Hitler's armies had swarmed over Yugoslavia and Greece, supporting Italian efforts in the Balkans. In June, Hitler launched his most audacious – and fateful – campaign of the whole war. Operation Barbarossa, the massive invasion of the USSR, tore up the truce established in the Molotov–Ribbentrop Pact. Under the cover of this push eastwards, the Nazis began the most terrible phase of the Holocaust (or Shoah): industrial genocide of European Jews. First, Jewish people were crammed into squalid, walled-off ghettos in cities like Warsaw; then, the mechanized murder began, in camps such as Auschwitz and Treblinka.

Away from Europe, in North Africa the two battles at El Alamein began an Allied grind towards regional victory. In November 1942, Anglo-American forces invaded Vichy-controlled Morocco and Algeria, laying the ground for an eventual push across the Mediterranean into southern Europe. After the Battle of Midway in June, the USA could envisage naval supremacy in the Pacific. When Soviet forces began counter-attacking at Stalingrad, from November 1942, Hitler was stretched on two fronts, against two rising superpowers. For the Allies, the end of 1942 suggested that the tide was turning. And on Guadalcanal, where Ralph Morse had spent a hair-raising Christmas, US troops were pushing towards victory.

Lend-Lease

On 11 March 1941, photographers clustered around President Roosevelt's desk in the White House to see him sign the 'Act to Promote the Defense of the United States'. Better known as the Lend-Lease Act, it edged the USA away from neutrality by allowing the government to provide friendly nations with 'defense articles' – food, fuel, weapons, vehicles and ships – on the understanding that this was also vital to the security of the USA.

The nations favoured by this act were all (eventually) on the Allied side: Britain, the French outside Vichy who fought on, China and the USSR. Lend-Lease answered the desperate need for the Allies to call freely on the US economy's vast resources, and to do so on long-term credit (Britain's final repayment on Lend-Lease supplies from the Second World War was made as recently as 2006). In February 1941, Churchill had made a ringing plea: 'Give us the tools, and we will finish the job!' Roosevelt's signature on the Lend-Lease Act answered that call.

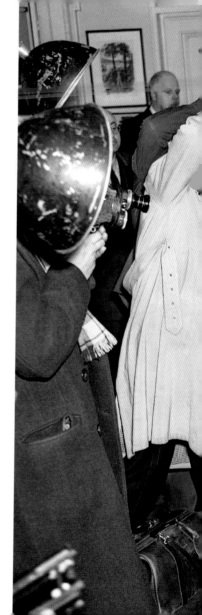

Free France

Among those who benefited from Lend-Lease were the *Forces françaises libres* – or Free French – under their leader, Charles de Gaulle, a First World War veteran who in 1916 had been captured and made a German prisoner of war for nearly three years. When France surrendered to the Nazis in 1940, de Gaulle was in London. He broadcast a speech on BBC radio, later summarized on propaganda posters as 'France has lost a battle, but France has not lost the war!'

De Gaulle initially commanded just a few thousand French troops; most of those Frenchmen evacuated at Dunkirk had returned home in June 1940. But the Free French included volunteers from among expatriates in Britain, and a women's corps too, led by Simonne Mathieu and modelled on Britain's Auxiliary Territorial Service. In this photograph from 1941, some of the *Corps féminin des volontaires françaises* march from the Free French HQ in London's Carlton Gardens. A contemporary report noted that they carried themselves with 'the spirit of Joan of Arc'. On their lapels is the Cross of Lorraine – the Free French insignia.

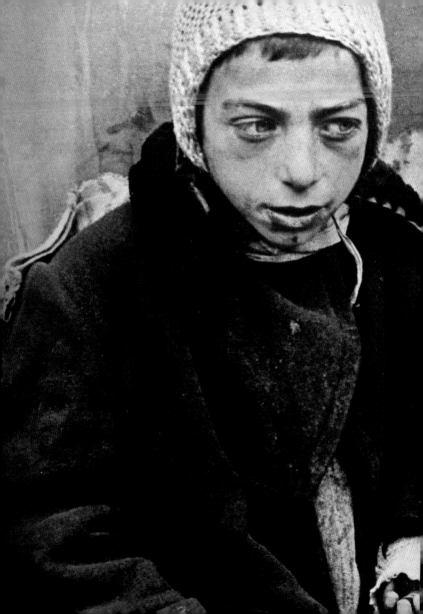

The Warsaw Ghetto

Wherever the Nazis conquered, they established an apparatus of oppression in the form of concentration camps, death camps and urban ghettos. The most notorious ghetto was in Warsaw, where these ragged and vulnerable children were photographed.

The Warsaw Ghetto was built in the autumn of 1940, as the Nazi occupiers forced the city's Jews to construct 3-metre (10-foot)-high walls around an area of the city measuring less than 2 square miles. Around 450,000 Jews would be imprisoned within these walls, in appalling conditions. Daily rations amounted to fewer than 200 calories per person. Typhus and other diseases connected to unsanitary conditions were rife. Medical supplies were limited. German war profiteers running sweatshops used the ghetto inhabitants for cheap or slave labour.

By July 1942, the Nazis had begun removing Jews from the ghetto. This 'resettlement' was in fact mass murder: Jews were packed in their thousands on trains, taking them to be killed in the gas chambers of Treblinka.

Alan Turing

By 1942 the Allies knew that behind German lines, millions of Jews were being murdered, both by roving SS death squads and in extermination camps. They discovered this because they could decode intercepted Nazi communications, a task that was spearheaded by Britain's 'Government Code & Cipher School' (GC&CS), based at Bletchley Park. Here, several thousand analysts made sense of encrypted enemy messages, including those sent using the Enigma machine, which the Nazis believed to be impossible to crack.

Alan Turing, photographed here, was one of Bletchley Park's most distinguished employees. For a time, he was in charge of 'Hut 8', a department that focused on cracking German naval communications sent using Enigma. Turing also spent some of the war working on voice encryption systems. After the war he was a pioneer of early computer design. He was prosecuted in 1952 for his homosexuality, accepted chemical castration as a punishment, and died two years later of cyanide poisoning, aged just forty-one. His status as an unfairly persecuted war hero has only recently been widely acknowledged.

Operation Barbarossa

Throughout the first half of 1941, intelligence sources across the world briefed that the Nazis were amassing huge military forces in eastern Europe, near the borders of the USSR. It seemed clear to most other leaders that Hitler was planning to attack. The only person who did not seem to believe that war was imminent was Joseph Stalin. The Nazi invasion of the USSR, known as Operation Barbarossa, began on 22 June 1941, when some three and a half million German and Axis troops, supported by thousands of tanks and aircraft, swarmed onto Soviet territory. This photograph shows a German artillery observer watching a shell landing.

Barbarossa had been meticulously planned and it was ruthlessly delivered. German troops overwhelmed Soviet defenders in a matter of weeks, having been ordered to abandon the usual etiquette of war in a campaign of 'annihilation', in which 'subordinate' peoples and communists were to be eliminated. When Stalin finally accepted what was happening, he embraced the need for new allies. An unlikely alliance between the United States, Britain and the USSR was soon taking shape.

Pearl Harbor

On 7 December 1941, more than 350 bombers and fighters of the Imperial Japanese Navy Air Service screamed out of the sky and attacked the US Pacific Fleet at anchor in Pearl Harbor, Hawaii. No official warning was given of the attack. President Roosevelt did not exaggerate when he said that 7 December was 'a date which will live in infamy'. This photograph shows the USS *West Virginia* being doused by fireboats in the aftermath of the attack. Despite these efforts the battleship sank, with the loss of 106 lives. In the final reckoning, around 2,400 Americans were killed at Pearl Harbor.

On the same day, Japan also attacked US territories in the Philippines and Guam, and British imperial possessions in Malaya, Hong Kong and Singapore. This massive escalation of the war in the Pacific changed the shape of the Second World War. On 8 December Roosevelt declared war on Japan; three days later the USA and Germany were also at war. The Axis powers had at last awoken the American giant.

Japanese-American internment

Four months after Pearl Harbor, internment orders were issued against 'All Persons of Japanese Ancestry' on the US West Coast. As a result, 50,000 Japanese immigrants (known as *Issei*) and their 70,000 US-born descendants (*Nisei*) were forced to abandon or sell their homes, before being ferried to out-of-state 'relocation centres' in Idaho, Arkansas, Colorado or Wyoming. Effectively prison camps, these were secured by guard towers and perimeter fences.

The legal basis for this forced migration was President Roosevelt's Executive Order 9066, issued on 19 February 1942, which allowed the US military to designate zones 'from which any or all persons may be excluded'. Although the order did not specify Japanese Americans as its target, its provisions allowed the military wide discretion and its underlying purpose was clear.

Internment was a bitter experience. But it reflected a hysteria stirred up by the attack on Pearl Harbor. In early 1942 seven Japanese submarines were detected in Californian waters, spurring invasion fears.

Flying Tigers

Less than two weeks after Pearl Harbor, US airmen flew their first combat mission against Japanese enemies. But they were not regular US Air Force pilots; they were the Flying Tigers (more properly, the First American Volunteer Group), three fighter squadrons sent to help the Chinese Air Force defend strategically vital positions from Japanese conquest. They flew Curtiss P-40 Warhawk single-seat fighters – shown here painted with the Tigers' distinctive shark-head design on the nose – and their three squadrons were known as the 'Adam & Eves', the 'Panda Bears' (based in China) and 'Hell's Angels' (based in Burma).

On their first combat mission, on 19 December 1941, fighters from the Adam & Eves and Panda Bears intercepted ten Japanese bombers, downing at least four of them. During the seven months that followed, the Flying Tigers took part in more than fifty fights and brought down nearly 300 enemy aircraft. They were retired as a distinct unit on 4 July 1942, but their exploits soon became Hollywood material. A film starring John Wayne and Anna Lee was released in October 1942, titled variously as *Flying Tigers* and *Yanks Over the Burma Road*.

The Fall of Singapore

The Japanese were ascendant in the east during the first half of 1942. One of their most famous victories occurred on 15 February when the Japanese Army captured a crucial British military base at Singapore, taking around 80,000 British and Imperial prisoners of war: the largest single surrender of forces in British history. This photograph was taken that day. Singapore had been nicknamed the 'Gibraltar of the East', its strategic location considered vital for the Royal Navy's power in the east. Its loss was devastating for the British.

In December 1941, Japanese forces commanded by Lieutenant-General Tomoyuki Yamashita had moved into the Malay peninsula and were soon advancing steadily south towards Singapore. At the same time, air raids on the island itself began. By the start of February, the Japanese were ready to force an amphibious landing. After a battle lasting seven days, the British commander, Lieutenant-General Arthur Percival, was authorized to surrender. Thousands of prisoners of war were put to work in labour camps and died from their mistreatment, while ethnic Malays and Chinese were murdered in their thousands.

The Battle of Midway

By May 1942, Japanese conquests included Hong Kong, the Philippines, Guam, Thailand, Malaya and Singapore, along with the oil-rich Dutch East Indies (Indonesia) and much of Burma and New Guinea. But between 4 and 8 May the Japanese Navy suffered a serious setback at the Battle of the Coral Sea, which convinced them that the US Navy had to be knocked out in the Pacific.

The result was the Battle of Midway, fought near that tiny island between Hawaii and Japan on 4 June. The US fleet was heavily outnumbered, and the aircraft available included the slow and outmoded Douglas TBD Devastator torpedo-bombers photographed here. However, US intelligence had decoded Japanese radio transmissions and was able to anticipate enemy plans. When the battle began, waves of Douglas Dauntless dive-bombers sank four Japanese aircraft carriers.

Midway was a double failure for the Japanese. Not only were the losses terrible and humiliating, the US Navy was now a potent presence in the Pacific, with vastly greater resources soon to arrive in the theatre. It was a critical moment: Japan had lost the upper hand in the Pacific.

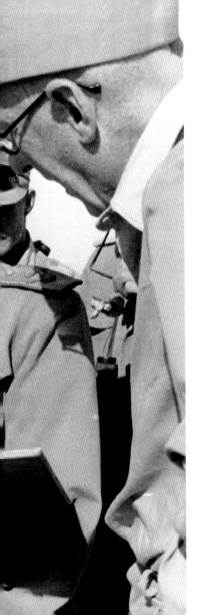

The Desert Fox

By the time the Second World War broke out, Erwin Rommel was one of the rising stars of the German military. His reputation beyond Germany was made from February 1941, when Hitler appointed him to lead the Panzer Army Africa (including the Afrika Korps), whose job was to save Italian Libya from the Allies. For nearly eighteen months he did just that, earning the nickname *Wüstenfuchs* or 'Desert Fox' and winning promotion to field marshal.

In this photograph, he (*left*) is liaising with the Italian commander Ettore Bastico; Rommel did not hold his Italian counterpart in very high regard. In 1943 the battle for North Africa would be lost and Rommel recalled to Europe, where he would help oversee work on the Atlantic Wall – sea defences to oppose a projected Allied invasion of France. When this invasion occurred – the D-Day landings of June 1944 – Rommel's car was strafed by an Allied fighter plane and he was badly injured. He was then implicated in the failed July 1944 plot to assassinate Hitler, and forced to commit suicide by taking cyanide.

The Dieppe Raid

This photograph, taken in August 1942, shows blindfolded Germans taken prisoner by Canadian forces. It appears to be a victorious moment for the Allies. Nothing could be further from the truth. Operation Jubilee, an amphibious assault on 19 August against the German-occupied Channel port of Dieppe, led by a largely Canadian expeditionary force, was in fact a fiasco in which German prisoners were few and far between.

The assault on Dieppe involved more than 230 vessels supported by RAF cover. But the Canadians were spotted by a German convoy before they reached their target, and were let down by inadequate intelligence. Ten hours after it had all begun, the remnants of the battered Allied force were limping back to Britain, with more than 900 Canadians killed and nearly 2,000 captured.

The Dieppe Raid was planned as a demonstration of aggressive Allied spirit, and as a fact-finding experience to help plan a full-scale invasion of France. It was a costly failure. But the lessons that were learned helped influence thinking about subsequent amphibious invasions of North Africa, later in 1942, and Normandy, in 1944.

The Battles of El Alamein

Although the Dieppe Raid was an exercise in failure, within weeks the Allies had a major victory to cheer elsewhere. In Egypt, the British Eighth Army – led by the prickly but brilliant Lieutenant-General Bernard Montgomery ('Monty') – struck decisively against German and Italian forces near El Alamein, removing the threat posed to the Middle East. Montgomery arrived to take command in Egypt in August 1942 and oversaw major investment in the Allied forces in the theatre. This photograph from 1942 shows Crusader II CS (close support) tanks, armed with howitzers. Swift and agile, these 'cruiser' tanks accompanied infantry into battle.

The Second Battle of El Alamein began on 23 October (the first had taken place in July). For around a week Rommel tried to coordinate resistance, but eventually yielded to overwhelming force, and on 4 November ordered a rapid retreat westwards, all the way across Libya into Tunisia. Behind him, 30,000 Axis troops were taken prisoner. In Britain, joy erupted. Monty and his Eighth Army were hailed as heroes. Church bells were rung across the nation, and Churchill called the victory the 'end of the beginning'.

Operation Torch

While the British were driving Rommel out of Egypt, on the other side of the continent a US-led amphibious invasion took aim at the Vichy French possessions of Morocco and Algeria. The invasion, code-named Operation Torch and commanded by Lieutenant-General Dwight D. Eisenhower, began on 8 November 1942. A secret armada of 650 warships landed at three points: two in Algeria and one in French Morocco. This photograph was taken by the Royal Navy photographer Lieutenant F. A. Hudson; it shows American troops of the Centre Task Force in a landing craft heading for the beaches of Oran, in Algeria.

Operation Torch met with limited opposition, thanks in part to careful measures that had been taken to disguise troop movements, and in part to a lack of sustained resistance by Vichy French fighters. After Operation Torch, Hitler ended Vichy's quasi-independence by occupying the whole of France. Meanwhile, Rommel found his northern African troops stuck in Tunisia, sandwiched between major Allied advances on either side. He prepared for a last stand, which would hold out until the spring of 1943.

Stalingrad

The dramatic clashes in North Africa during autumn 1942 were dwarfed by an elemental struggle that took place around the city of Stalingrad (modern Volgograd) at the same time. Hitler invaded the USSR expecting a swift victory. In fact, a long and bitter war developed and Stalingrad epitomized the worst of it. It was the biggest, deadliest and most dreadful engagement in the whole of the Second World War.

The assault began in August 1942: the Luftwaffe bombed much of Stalingrad into dust, while forces including German, Italian and Croatian troops stormed forwards. However, the city did not fall, and in November the Soviet Red Army launched Operation Uranus, which cut off around 250,000 Axis troops. This photograph shows a Soviet artillery crew in action. In early February 1943, the German commander, Field Marshal Friedrich Paulus, surrendered. It was a huge Soviet victory which began to turn the tide in the east. But nearly two million people had been killed, captured or injured in its pursuit.

Turning Points

I n the first days of July 1943, the land around the Russian city and railway junction at Kursk echoed with explosions and the roar of heavy machinery. Smoke and dust swirled. The ground shook from the blasts exchanged by massive German and Soviet forces. Vehicles smashed into one another and burst in giant fireballs. Aircraft in their thousands shrieked overhead. An astonishing two million troops were thrown, with increasing desperation, into a battle that lasted nearly two months. This image, taken during training exercises, shows four Red Army soldiers taking cover in a trench as a Soviet T-34 tank crawls across the shattered landscape above them. It was an experience designed to mimic the horrors of battles like this.

The Battle of Kursk was a pivotal clash on the Eastern Front. One of the biggest land battles ever fought, it also featured, in the sub-battle of Prokhorovka on 12 July, the largest clash of tanks in the Second World War, in which around 600 Soviet

T-34s took on half as many German tanks, swarming 'like rats' over the parched terrain, according to a German eyewitness.

The prelude to Kursk came in the winter of 1942–3, when the German Sixth Army and its allies had been trapped, bombed, starved and frozen into submission at Stalingrad. By the summer, Soviet advances and German counter-attacks resulted in a 150-mile (240km) Soviet bulge at Kursk, which was potentially vulnerable. Eventually, in June 1943 Hitler authorized Operation Citadel to attack it, on 5 July. It failed. Soviet intelligence had intercepted many of the planning details, allowing Stalin's men to plant mines and set up antitank defences. Within a fortnight, and amid mounting pressures elsewhere, Hitler cancelled Citadel; but on 12 July, a massive Soviet counter-attack began driving the Germans back, recovering the cities of Orel (Oryol) and Kharkov (Kharkiv, in Ukraine), which had been in enemy hands since 1941. By the time the Battle of Kursk was over, on 23 August, the balance of power on the Eastern Front had swung in favour of the USSR.

The T-34 tank, as seen here, played an important role in the Soviet successes. Its rounded contours and thick armour helped deflect enemy fire. It was agile, could travel at up to 33 miles per hour (53km/h) and was equipped with a powerful 76.2mm gun. German tanks included the heavily armoured and rapid Panther, with a 75mm gun, which debuted at Kursk, and the Tiger tank, which was twice the weight of a T-34 and equipped with armour up to 100mm thick, making it virtually impervious to frontal attack. Yet both these tanks were vulnerable when the lighter, nimbler T-34s got in and around them. Horrified eyewitnesses at Kursk would remember tanks crushed and mangled together, some firing at close – even point-blank – range, contributing their share of death to a battle where estimated casualties ran to more than a million men.

Men, though, was what the USSR had, in vast numbers. The decline of Nazi fortunes on the Eastern Front in 1943–4 owed much to the USSR's vast population and their willingness to suffer unimaginably high losses in defending the motherland. Yet Hitler was also stymied in the summer of 1943 by the Allied invasion of Sicily, forcing him to divert troops to Italy. On 25 July, 1943 Mussolini fell from power, setting in train events that would lead to the partition of Italy and a nasty guerrilla war.

Germany was suffering too in 1943, from an Anglo-American bomber offensive that sought to destroy industries, cities and morale. Allied bombing altogether killed half a million people in Germany. But it was not enough to cripple the Nazi regime, which continued to commit its crimes against humanity in ghettoes and death camps across Europe.

At a conference in Tehran, Allied leaders decided when their long-anticipated landings in France would take place. The day eventually came on 6 June 1944: D-Day, the largest amphibious military landing ever carried out. It was far from the final act in a war that had many dreadful chapters still to be written – not least in the islands of the Pacific Ocean. All the same, it was the beginning of the end for Hitler and his Axis partners.

Charles de Gaulle

When this photograph was taken, on 31 March 1943, General Charles de Gaulle was in London, the city he had reluctantly made his home since the fall of France nearly three years previously. De Gaulle was not entirely gracious in his exile. He referred to the British and Americans as the 'Anglo Saxons', and his relationships with Churchill and Roosevelt often verged on being openly hostile. Nevertheless, de Gaulle occupied a rare status among those working to free France. Here, he is meeting young volunteers from the islands of Saint-Pierre and Miquelon – a tiny outpost of French territory off the coast of Newfoundland, which had been liberated from Vichy rule in 1941.

At this point, de Gaulle's residence in Britain was nearly over. Operation Torch had now liberated former Vichy French colonial territories in North Africa, and in May 1943 he moved his headquarters to Algiers, elbowed aside his US-backed rival General Henri Giraud and took sole charge of a new provisional government of Free France. He would remain a dominant force in French politics until 1969.

The Warsaw Ghetto Uprising

During the summer of 1942, Nazi rulers deported a quarter of a million Jewish people from the Warsaw Ghetto to be murdered at Treblinka. By the following spring, no more than 60,000 Jews remained. Increasingly desperate, they began to form resistance groups and to improvise underground bunkers.

On 19 April 1943, the eve of Passover, the SS officer and local police commander Jürgen Stroop (*centre, looking up*) led an effort to remove the last inhabitants of the ghetto. He was faced with massive opposition. The flags of Poland and the ZZW (Jewish Military Union) were raised defiantly over the rooftops, and insurgents attacked the police with Molotov cocktails and smuggled guns.

Stroop responded by ordering his men to set fire to the ghetto and dynamite all the bunkers and tunnel networks. It took until 16 May to suppress the rebellion. Afterwards, Stroop composed a report of his actions, illustrated by photographs including this one. He was hanged in 1952 for crimes against humanity.

The Dambusters

Although the Allies were briefed about the atrocities at Auschwitz, the British and American high command decided not to bomb the Nazi death camps. Instead, throughout 1943 they concentrated air power on German industrial targets. On 16–17 May 1943 the RAF's 617 Squadron undertook a daring – and now legendary – mission to destroy dams in the Ruhr Valley, known as Operation Chastise. Their commanding officer was twenty-four-year-old Guy Gibson, photographed here a month after the raid.

In this image, Gibson is showing an aerial photograph of the Möhne dam, one of three targeted by the 'Dambusters'. As can be seen, the wall was successfully breached. This caused floodwater to sweep through the valley below, killing around 1400 people (many of them slave labourers in Nazi factories), washing away buildings, roads and bridges, and crippling steel production. After the raid, Gibson was awarded the Victoria Cross and briefly became a celebrity. He was killed in September 1944 when his plane crashed in the Netherlands, while he was returning from a combat mission.

MOHNE DAM

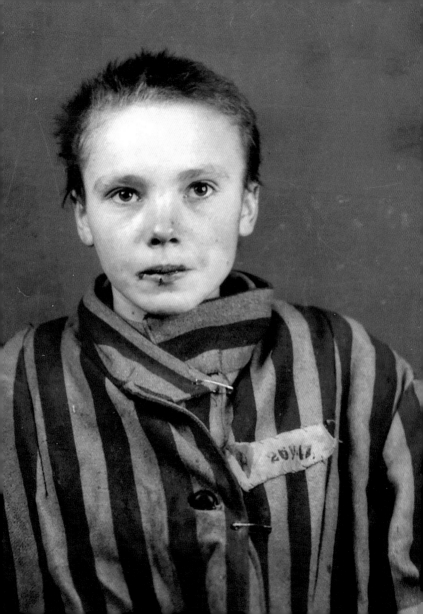

Auschwitz-Birkenau

Czesława Kwoka was born on 15 August 1928 in Wólka Złojecka, a small Polish village occupied by the Nazis in 1939. Like her mother Katarzyna, Czesława was a Roman Catholic; their village had been earmarked for ethnic cleansing ahead of future German resettlement and on 13 December 1942 both were deported to Auschwitz.

The Auschwitz-Birkenau camp complex was created in spring 1940. In March 1942 industrial-scale murder of Jews in gas chambers began. During the Second World War, 1.1 million Jews, 140,000 non-Jewish Poles, 23,000 Roma, 15,000 Soviet prisoners of war and 25,000 other people were killed there. They included both Katarzyna, who died on 18 February 1943, and Czesława, who was murdered a month later with a phenol injection to the heart. She was fourteen years old. These images of Czesława – showing a cut on her lip from a beating by an overseer – were taken by another Polish prisoner, Wilhelm Brasse, a professional photographer forced to take 'identity photographs'.

Sicily

The *Life* photographer Bob Landry came ashore at Gela in Sicily a few hours before dawn, on the moonless night of 9–10 July 1943. He was accompanying US troops landing in the first wave of Operation Husky, the Allied invasion of Sicily. Machine-gun fire raked the sands as the American landing craft arrived, and Landry and the men he was shadowing had to scramble for cover across uncleared minefields. Over the course of the next forty-eight hours Landry watched and photographed heavy fighting in and around Gela.

Landry took this picture on the Via Pisa, near the town hall, where US troops had set up a machine gun on a marble monument commemorating two Italian heroes of the First World War, lauded in the monument's epigram as 'Fascist martyrs' who had later died defending Mussolini's 'new Empire of Rome'. Yet Mussolini's new Rome was about to fall. Within three weeks of the landings at Gela, Allied troops had taken around 80 per cent of the island and were preparing to push north into mainland Italy.

Fascism Floundering

On the evening of 25 July 1943, Benito Mussolini visited King Victor Emmanuel III at the Villa Savoia in Rome to discuss the crisis in Sicily. The night before, Mussolini had lost the support of his Grand Council of Fascism. Now the king told him he was to be removed from power altogether. In his place, Marshal Pietro Badoglio – a veteran of both world wars and the Italian campaigns in Libya and Abyssinia – was appointed prime minister. The next day, 26 July, these workmen were smashing away the Fascist insignia from Rome's Ministry of Finance.

In the south, Allied forces were readying to invade the mainland – a campaign that began on 3 September and resulted in the signing of an armistice that was made public five days later. But Hitler would not allow his Axis partner to melt from the theatre of war. German troops were already deploying through Italy, with the aim of stopping the Allies in the south and creating a Nazi puppet state in the north. Fascism was not quite dead.

The Lancaster Bomber

The Avro Lancaster first flew in 1941. By the summer of 1943, this four-engined strategic bomber, which took off with a crew of seven men and had a range of more than 2,500 miles (4,000km), was the standard aircraft deployed by RAF Bomber Command to attack cities, railways, roads and factories across Nazi Germany. Lancasters were used by the 'Dambusters' in May 1943; and between July 1943 and March 1944 hundreds of them bombed Hamburg, Berlin and Bremen, killing tens of thousands of German civilians, making many more homeless and reducing Hamburg in particular to ruins.

The Lancaster here is a B Mark 1, flown by RAF 207 Squadron, who were based in Nottinghamshire. On 13 September 1943 it was destined for Bremen, and its open doors reveal a deadly payload known as a 'usual': one 4,000lb (1,814kg) 'cookie' bomb surrounded by incendiaries, and four 250lb (113kg) target indicators. By the end of the war, modified Lancasters could drop yet larger and more destructive devices, capable of sinking a battleship. Like the Spitfire, the Lancaster became an icon, symbolic of the British war effort.

Operation Tidal Wave

The German Reich was not the only target for Allied air raids in 1943. This photograph shows a Consolidated B-24 Liberator of the US Army Air Force taking part in one of a series of bombing missions in 1943–4 designed to disrupt oil refineries at Ploeşti, in Romania. The heaviest – and costliest – of these raids was known as Operation Tidal Wave, and it took place on Sunday 1 August 1943.

Romania's oil fields were critical to the Axis war effort: nearly a third of the oil needed to fuel vehicles and supply vital industries came from the country. But attacking Ploeşti was extremely difficult: there were hundreds of anti-aircraft guns around the oil fields, and Romanian fighter planes were stationed nearby, ready to scramble. When 177 US bombers arrived at Ploeşti, having taken off from their base near Benghazi, in Libya, they faced fierce resistance from both air and ground. Alhough many bombers landed direct hits on the refineries, only eighty-eight aircraft made it back to Benghazi. The USAAF lost 310 airmen killed; another 190 were captured. Romanian oil output soon recovered, and 1 August was later nicknamed 'Black Sunday'.

The Battle for Tarawa

While US airmen bombed eastern Europe, US Marines were engaged in a different, very brutal war in the central Pacific, fighting troops of the Imperial Japanese Navy. One of these clashes, pictured here, was the Battle of Tarawa Atoll, part of the Gilbert Islands (modern Kiribati). Most of the fighting, between 20 and 23 November 1943, took place on the island of Betio, just two miles in length and a few hundred metres wide. Yet although Betio was tiny, it was heavily reinforced by 4,500 Japanese with artillery, deep bunkers and concealed machine-gun positions.

In the end, it took 18,000 Marines about seventy-six hours to take Betio, but at the cost of more than 3,000 casualties. The Japanese fought, quite literally, to the death: just seventeen defenders survived to be captured at the end of the battle. The human cost of taking Betio shocked the American public, who were exceptionally well informed thanks to magazine reporting, photojournalism and an Oscar-winning documentary of the battle, *With the Marines at Tarawa*.

The Tehran Conference

A war with so many belligerents fighting on so many fronts demanded clear thinking about overall strategy, so in late November 1943, two major leaders' conferences were convened. One took place in Cairo, where Chiang Kai-shek met Churchill and Roosevelt. The second, pictured here, was held from 28 November to 1 December in Tehran, Iran. It was the first meeting between Churchill, Roosevelt and Joseph Stalin.

Stalin disliked travelling outside the USSR, but on this occasion he did so out of necessity. The Red Army had been fighting long and hard on Europe's Eastern Front, and the Soviet leader wanted the Allies to open a second front. In a lighter vein, Stalin toasted Churchill as his 'fighting friend' while Churchill conveyed to Stalin a ceremonial sword from King George VI for the 'steel-hearted citizens of Satlingrad'. By the end of the meeting, several major issues had been settled. Stalin agreed to declare war on Japan following the defeat of Germany, while the Western leaders agreed a date of May 1944 for Operation Overlord – the invasion of France.

Chiang Kai-shek

A little over a month after the Chinese nationalist leader Chiang Kai-shek met the Allied leaders in Cairo, he was in India's north-eastern Bihar province, addressing Chinese troops – the scene depicted in this photograph. The terms concluded in Cairo were promising: the Allies had agreed to stand together to oppose Japanese expansion in the Pacific and return to China all lands surrendered to Japan since the end of the First World War.

In theory, Chiang was the Allies' most important man in the Far East, carrying the titles Generalissimo and Supreme Allied Commander in China. His wife, Soong Mei-ling (or 'Madame Chiang' to Westerners), was American-educated and a popular figure in the United States, where she rallied support for the Chinese cause and was featured on the cover of *Time* magazine. Yet Chiang needed close Allied backing to bolster his position in his sprawling, fragmented nation, assisting him against the Japanese invaders but also against his internal enemy, the Chinese communists. Without US money, training, warplanes and air cargoes, his cause would have been in a parlous state.

'X Force'

Artillery captain Huang Cheun-yu of the Chinese Expeditionary Force's Sixth Army, New 22nd Division, was photographed in Burma in April 1944 (for *Life* magazine). Part of the British Empire, Burma had been captured by the Japanese in 1942, cutting off the main supply route between India and China known as the 'Burma Road'. It now fell to men like Captain Huang and their British and American allies to try to fight their way back through Burma, opening a new route: the Ledo Road. Those Chinese troops who undertook this mission from the Indian side of Burma were known as 'X Force'. (Those who approached from the Chinese border were 'Y Force'.) They had been trained by American military advisors, at British expense, and were often accompanied on the ground by US Special Forces.

In contrast with soldiers on the Chinese mainland, who were often abjectly treated and miserably equipped, men of the X Force such as Captain Huang benefitted from modern weaponry, proper shoes and boots, steel helmets, and instruction in skills as diverse as operating radios to firing artillery, as well as superior medical care, welfare and sustenance.

The Battle of Anzio

By the beginning of 1944, Italy had been partitioned. The official government had agreed an armistice with the Allies. But the north of the country was now a Nazi puppet state, called the Italian Social Republic. Rome was under occupation and German defensive lines stretched across the Italian peninsula.

On 22 January 1944, the Allies attempted to storm ashore midway between those lines, landing nearly 400 vessels in and around Anzio, a seaside resort just south of Rome. This photograph, taken by the *Life* photographer George Silk, shows US GIs of the 3rd Infantry a week following the first landings, shepherding captured German infantrymen to a confinement centre after fighting near Cisterna. But despite this snapshot of American success, Anzio was not a swift, Sicilian-style victory. Rather, it was a long, gruelling battle that produced more than 80,000 casualties across all sides. Old fashioned, attritional warfare meant it took four months between the landings and the breakthrough in early June that allowed the Allies finally to advance on Rome.

Operation Overlord

As the Allies in Italy laboured towards Rome, in Britain the long-anticipated invasion of northern France was nearing readiness. Operation Overlord involved over two million servicemen from more than a dozen countries, directed by the Allied Supreme Commander, Dwight D. Eisenhower. He is pictured here on the evening of 5 June 1944, the day before the invasion, meeting US paratroopers of the 502nd Parachute Infantry Regiment at Greenham Common, Berkshire.

Despite the pressure, Eisenhower showed his humanity: Lieutenant Walter C. Strobel, pictured here wearing the '23' label (indicating the line of parachute-jumpers for whom he was responsible), remembered talking to the general about fly fishing.

The target of Overlord was the beaches of Normandy, code-named Gold, Juno, Sword, Omaha and Utah. When the invasion came, these men were dropped from the air behind 'Utah' and detailed to seize gun batteries and two causeways. Strobel survived; many others did not.

D-Day

From the small hours of 6 June almost 7,000 ships and landing craft crossed the choppy English Channel and around 160,000 soldiers leaped out of them, into the cold sea and on to the Normandy beaches. Ten thousand Allied aircraft swept the skies above, while naval guns blasted German defences dug into the shoreline. The military called this first day of Operation Overlord 'D-Day'.

This photograph, known as 'Into the Jaws of Death', was taken on the approach to Omaha beach by US Coast Guard photographer Robert F. Sargent. The men shown wading ashore are from the 16th Infantry, US 1st Infantry Division, who had been transported to the beach from the USS *Samuel Chase* on an 'LCVP' (Landing Craft, Vehicle, Personnel). The fighting they were about to encounter was some of the fiercest in all of the landings. Several thousand men were killed or wounded and it took until the next day to secure the whole of Omaha beach. But despite such hardships, D-Day succeeded. The Allied invasion of France had begun.

1944–1945

Liberation

$\int$ ix months after D-Day, hundreds of thousands of Allied troops were pushing through occupied France and northwest Europe. After facing stiff German resistance during the summer, their advance was now proceeding rapidly, and there were many reasons for Allied optimism. Hitler's resources were tautly stretched and his armies undermanned; the USSR was preparing a winter assault; regular Allied strikes on Romanian oil fields were drying up fuel supplies, and the Allies now had massive air superiority over France. The Führer's only chance of rescuing his fortunes would be through enormous strategic gambles. The result was a five-week campaign fought in and around the forests of the Ardennes, best known to history as the 'Battle of the Bulge'.

This photograph of a weary and wounded German soldier was taken by the American *Life* photographer John Florea during that battle. Before the war he had snapped celebrities. But in

December 1944, his posting with the US First Army thrust him into this battle, the biggest and deadliest fought by US troops during the whole of the Second World War. For what Churchill called 'the greatest American victory of the war', US forces traded 80,000 casualties.

Hitler's gamble was to throw everything he could muster into the Ardennes, in the hope that he could punch a hole in Allied lines and perhaps recapture their main supply port at Antwerp. He knew that US and British troops in France were tired and running dangerously low on supplies. If they were split and seriously beaten in this northern sector, Hitler reasoned, then there was a chance of negotiating a peace with the Western powers, allowing him to concentrate on battling the USSR. That this was largely fantasy was immaterial. On 16 December, amid heavy snowstorms in the Ardennes, his generals commenced their attack.

The initial shock and speed of the assault caught the thinly spread US troops by surprise. The ferocity of this offensive allowed the Germans to push a large, triangle-shaped bulge into Allied lines around the Belgian towns of St Vith and Bastogne. After initial successes, however, the German advance began to fail. Chronic fuel shortages, along with the Allies' ability both to commit large numbers of reinforcements and to take advantage of the tough terrain, meant that by late January 1945, US forces had regained all the territory lost in December.

Florea documented the hard fighting with terrifying clarity. Besides this photograph (the young man here was wounded while trying to attack an American fuel depot), he also captured the horrifying sight of the 'Malmédy massacre' of 17 December, in which around 150 unarmed US prisoners were gunned down in cold blood by SS troopers. Though by this time an experienced war photographer, Florea later recalled: 'I felt someone had hit me so hard – I actually cried. It was the most shocking thing I had ever seen.'

Such vengeful atrocities could not conceal the reality that in 1944 the Führer's war was collapsing everywhere. Italy was slowly being prized out of Fascist hands. The Nazis abandoned Vichy France. Soviet forces sent German armies reeling back across Belorussia and Poland to Warsaw; they also penetrated the Baltic States, and forced Romania, Bulgaria and Finland to swap sides, while besieging the Hungarian capital, Budapest. German control of Yugoslavia, Greece and Albania collapsed. Hitler, ever more isolated from his people, his generals and reality, demanded fights to the death and scorched earth strategies. In July, a plot to assassinate him narrowly failed. On 25 August, the liberation of Paris was a moment of triumph for many of its citizens, though for others accused of collaboration with the Nazi occupiers it ushered in rituals of retribution.

Meanwhile, far away in the Pacific, US Marines won critical battles on the island of Saipan and in the Philippine Sea, although they faced enemies who embraced death and strove to take the maximum number of enemy lives as they did so. Just as 'doodlebug' pilotless bombs and V2 supersonic rockets created havoc in the west, so suicidal kamikaze pilots were a bane in the east. The weapons of war were becoming more ingenious. And worse, and far more destructive, was still to come.

Cherbourg

As Allied forces worked to secure the Normandy beaches during the hours and days after D-Day, the US VII Corps were sent to take control of Normandy's Cotentin Peninsula and its port of Cherbourg. By 21 June, the US forces were on the town's perimeter, and for the next week they fought in the streets and suburbs, while US and British naval guns fired at the coastal defences.

On 26 June the German commander of Cherbourg's garrison, Lieutenant-General Karl Wilhelm von Schlieben (*centre*), surrendered, to the joy of Cherbourg's inhabitants and to the disgust of Hitler, who pronounced him a 'disgrace'. By contrast, Hitler awarded Rear-Admiral Walter Hennecke (*far right*) the Knight's Cross for having ordered the deliberate destruction of port facilities in Cherbourg before the city fell. This photograph shows von Schlieben being escorted off a landing craft onto British soil. Both von Schlieben and Hennecke were imprisoned in Britain until the end of the war before being sent home to Germany.

The Battle of the Hedgerows

Fighting their way through Normandy, Allied soldiers discovered that the characteristic local landscape of narrow sunken lanes, surrounded by banks and thick hedgerows – known as *bocage* – could be a deathtrap. The nature of this Norman *bocage* made it perfect territory for concealment and ambush; hidden machine guns could spray a column of marching men; tanks could lurk around any corner, camouflaged by trees or tangles of vegetation. During the summer months of 1944, therefore, a sort of guerrilla-style war developed, as US and British troops adapted their own tactics – and equipment – to the local surroundings.

These US soldiers are firing a 105mm HM2 howitzer, which they have disguised under camouflage netting. The men pictured were fighting around Saint-Lô, where one of the most ferocious encounters of the Normandy campaign took place. The town was considered strategically vital to securing lower Normandy, and heavy bombardment added to damage that had been done earlier in the war. Saint-Lô was taken for the Allies between 7 and 19 July, but virtually the entire city was left desolate.

'Doodlebugs'

Unmanned flying 'V-1' bombs of the type pictured here were known in German as *Vergeltungswaffe 1* or 'Revenge Weapon 1'. To ordinary Britons they were 'buzz bombs' or 'doodlebugs'. The first were launched on 13 June 1944, and their purpose was straightforward: to fly across the Channel from launch sites in occupied France and the Low Countries, and fall wherever their engines ran out of fuel, blowing up whatever (or whoever) they landed upon.

The noise made by a doodlebug overhead – a pulsing drone – was unnerving. More troubling still was the engine falling silent, since this meant that the bomb was soon to crash-land and detonate. Although doodlebugs killed more than 6,000 people in Britain, many veered off course, while fighter planes and anti-aircraft guns became increasingly adept at shooting them down. By the time this damaged V-1 was displayed in London, on 31 October 1944, smiles were justified, for the danger was largely over. Unfortunately, in the meantime, the Nazis had developed a new weapon – the V-2. This was a supersonic rocket that plunged to earth without warning and without possibility of interception.

Operation Valkyrie

Despite the development of weapons like the V-1, by mid-July 1944 it was evident to many in the German high command that the war situation was dire. Among some high-ranking German officers, Hitler's leadership was now seen as a grave impediment to any hope of avoiding national catastrophe. As early as the winter of 1942–3, Army dissidents had been considering a plot to assassinate the Führer. By the summer of 1944 this plan, codenamed Operation Valkyrie, was ready for execution.

On 20 July one of the plotters, Colonel Claus von Stauffenberg, joined Hitler's conference in his East Prussian bunker complex, the *Wolfsschanze* (Wolf's Lair). Von Stauffenberg was a disillusioned officer who had served the Reich well, and bore the scars to prove it: an amputated hand and an eye patch. Having brought a bomb into the room in a briefcase, von Stauffenberg left the room and the device exploded. But the briefcase had been moved, and a solid oak table support protected Hitler. Within 24 hours, von Stauffenberg was shot by a firing squad. Other plotters committed suicide or were captured.

The Liberation of Paris

The plotters who failed to kill Hitler were not the only Nazis convinced that the Führer no longer deserved their obedience. In Paris, the commander of the German garrison, Dietrich von Choltitz, had concluded, as he later put it, that 'Hitler was insane'. As Allied troops approached the French capital in the middle of August 1944, von Choltitz had a choice to make. He could follow Hitler's orders, which were to burn and bomb the city to the ground, or he could surrender the streets to the French Resistance.

The day for deciding was not long coming. With the Allies advancing out of Normandy, on 15 August Parisians rose in readiness for liberation. On the night of 24/25 August, General Philippe Leclerc led the French 2nd Armoured Division into Paris; here they are seen being greeted by crowds on a corner of the rue Guynemer. Behind them came the US 4th Infantry Division. Von Choltitz formally – and sensibly – surrendered on 25 August at the Hôtel Meurice. After four years, Paris was free.

Americans in Paris

Along with the fighters came the reporters. The liberation of Paris was a historic moment, irresistible to men like two of those pictured here. On the left is the photo-journalist Robert Capa, often ranked as the greatest war photographer of all time. Capa had been in the Spanish Civil War in 1937, the Japanese invasion of China in 1938 and in Naples during the Allied invasion of Italy in 1943. He was in Paris on 25 August, photographing stand-offs as soldiers and Parisians sheltered in doorways and behind barricades.

On the other side of a driver (*centre*) is Ernest Hemingway (*right*), who was reporting from France for *Collier's* magazine. On 25 August he rushed to Paris, celebrating French freedom with champagne at the Travellers' Club, before heading to 'liberate' the Ritz Hotel, where his group was said to have run up a bill for fifty-one martinis. Despite Hemingway's fondness for the idea of himself as a great war reporter, he was in fact far better at drinking and showing off, unlike his wife of the time, Martha Gellhorn, a far more talented and serious correspondent.

Operation Dragoon

As Paris fell, Allied troops landed at beaches in southern France. Although planned to coincide with D-Day, Operation Dragoon was ultimately delayed until the beachheads in Normandy had been secured. The landings began on 15 August, when US, French and Canadian forces converged on France's Mediterranean coast from bases in Italy, Corsica and Algeria. This photograph shows civilians literally kicking the German occupiers out of Toulon. By 14 September, German forces had abandoned the French south altogether and retreated to the Vosges mountains. Marshal Pétain and the Vichy government were sent to become a government-in-exile in the southern German town of Sigmaringen.

If the collapse of Vichy France was swift, it was nonetheless violent. In the weeks and months before D-Day, Nazi officials had carried out revenge attacks against civilians and the resistance fighters known as the *Maquis*, who also battled the Vichy paramilitary *Milice*. After Allied liberation, many ex-*miliciens* were subjected to official treason proceedings and unofficial beatings and executions.

Collaboration and Shame

Reprisals across France were notably severe against women accused of *collaboration horizontale* – sleeping with the enemy. Throughout France, from Brittany to Provence, an estimated 20,000 women were subjected to a ritualized form of ostracization for consorting with Germans: their hair was shaved off in public. Some were then daubed with swastikas and stripped to their underwear, before being paraded through the streets.

This process – seen taking place here – was known as a *carnival moche*, 'ugly carnival', and it was a method of publicly shaming women that had a grievously long European history. It had its roots in the Middle Ages, when it was sometimes used as punishment for adultery, but the ritual had been revived throughout Europe during the world wars. Needless to say, this rough and misogynistic form of mob justice often targeted women who were unable to defend themselves, or who had been the victims of unhappy or impossible circumstances. It was barely policed by the liberating armies.

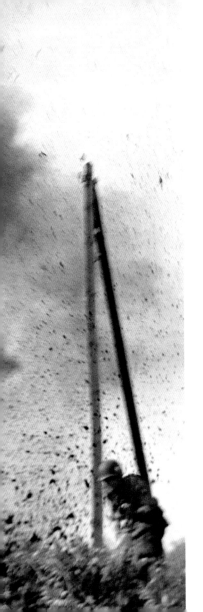

Operation Market-Garden

Liberating Paris was strategically less important than the drive towards Germany. The Allies had to find a way to deal with the Siegfried Line or *Westwall*: defensive fortifications stretching along the German border between Switzerland and the Netherlands. Field Marshal Montgomery developed an ambitious plan to circumvent the *Westwall*. It resulted in scenes like this, in which US paratroopers narrowly evade a shell burst in a soggy Dutch field.

On 17 September 1944, two US airborne divisions, one British and the Polish Parachute Brigade dropped into occupied Holland. The goal of Operation Market was to secure bridges over the Meuse and Lower Rhine tributaries and hold them long enough for the British XXX Corps to arrive overland (Operation Garden), consolidate the gains, and open a path into Germany's industrial heartland.

Initial success soon faded. British paratroopers landed short of the furthest bridge, at Arnhem; Allied equipment went astray; and XXX Corps were slowed down by fighting, the difficult landscape and bad weather. Arnhem was lost, as were three-quarters of the British troops, mostly captured.

The Ruins of Aachen

With the failure of Operation Market-Garden, there was little choice for the Allies but to press on with a slow and steady direct advance on Germany. On 21 October 1944, US forces captured Aachen, the country's westernmost city and a place of deep historical resonance. When they entered the city, much of it lay in ruins. Hitler's orders for defence of the Reich betrayed ruthless intent: where Germany could not be defended, everything of value should be destroyed before the invaders could claim it.

This photograph was taken in Aachen's ancient cathedral. In the ninth century, Aachen was the seat of power for Charlemagne's Frankish empire, and his Palatine Chapel, now part of the cathedral, became the emperor's resting place. For hundreds of years afterwards, German kings were crowned in the chapel, to which the choir, seen here, was added in the thirteenth century.

These US serviceman, gazing up from the rubble-strewn floor, would have been unable to appreciate the vibrant colours once thrown by the stained-glass windows, which gave the choir the name *Glashaus*. It took two years from 1949 to restore the glories of the *Glashaus*.

Greek Liberation

In 1941 Greece had been swiftly conquered by German and Italian armies. On 27 April of that year, the swastika had flown above the Acropolis – the birthplace of democracy – and the country had been partitioned between the Axis powers. When Italy fell to the Allies in 1943, Nazi control had been extended over most of Greece. The occupation had caused widespread misery and hardship so there was jubilation when, in October 1944, German troops abandoned Athens. This photograph shows a parade in the Greek capital, with citizens celebrating in traditional dress.

However, these celebrations masked political strife. In December 1944, rioting broke out in Athens, and a civil war was soon underway. This pitted the Greek government, backed by British troops, against Greek communists, who were encouraged from afar by men like Josip Broz 'Tito', the Yugoslav revolutionary leader. Although it was eventually won by the Western-backed government, civil war would plague Greece until the end of the 1940s.

Sapian

The Allies were keen to defeat Germany as quickly as possible so that they could concentrate their efforts on Japan in the east. That became a real possibility from the summer of 1944 after a ferocious battle between US Marines and the Imperial Japanese Army on the island of Saipan – one of the Northern Mariana Islands, not far from Guam.

Saipan was a vital target for US forces, because it could serve as a launch pad for air raids, putting Toyko within reach of new American long-range B-29 Superfortress bomber planes. The Japanese, under Lieutenant-General Yoshitsugu Saitō, were determined to defend it to the death. On 15 June 1944, 600 US landing craft arrived and three weeks' hard struggle began, during which thousands of civilians died. This photograph shows US Marines treating a wounded child on Saipan. It was taken by W. Eugene Smith, who covered many of the campaigns in the Pacific for *Life* magazine (and later lived for a time with his wife in Japan). On 7 July, the last 3,000-odd Japanese soldiers staged a mass *banzai* suicide attack. Saitō ritually disembowelled himself.

Kamikaze

All the men pictured here intended to commit suicide. They are *kamikaze* pilots. The word, meaning 'divine wind', evoked a typhoon that saved Japan from a Mongol invasion fleet in 1281. Six and a half centuries later, in autumn 1944, Japanese Rear Admiral Masafumi Arima created *kamikaze* culture when he crashed his Yokosuka D4Y divebomber into a US aircraft carrier, killing himself but damaging the vessel in the process. Arima's example was used to promote the concept of honourable suicide in the service of emperor and the homeland.

Kamikaze attacks began at the Battle of Leyte Gulf (23–26 October 1944), during the recapture of the Philippines. On 25 October, the USS *St. Lo*, a small aircraft carrier, was the first US vessel sunk by *kamikaze* action. On this occasion, *kamikaze* tactics were not enough to avert another disaster for the Japanese, who lost twenty-seven ships. But the *kamikaze* programme was just beginning. By 1945, suicide pilots would be flying 'cherry blossoms': rocket-powered piloted torpedoes.

The Lapland War

Far away from the Pacific, in the scrub and tundra of the Arctic Circle, came a new twist in the war. In October 1944, Soviet winter troops like these were fighting in Finnish Lapland – on the side of the Finns. This represented a major shift in alliances. Three years earlier, in 1941, matters had been very different: a deal had been struck between Nazi Germany and a group of senior Finnish politicians, by which Finland would invade Russian territory at the same time as the Wehrmacht. From that summer, therefore, Finland was at war with the USSR, in a conflict known as the Continuation War.

The Continuation War ended in September 1944, having cost by that point around one million casualties. However, the deal that ended hostilities, known as the Moscow Armistice, demanded that Finnish troops remove every trace of the German military presence from their borders. For the next seven months, therefore, Finnish troops with Soviet backup were engaged in chasing German units through Lapland towards Nazi-occupied Norway. By April 1945, the retreat – and the war – was over.

The Race to Berlin

By the time these Soviet artillerymen were dragging a field gun across the River Oder, around 31 January 1945, the end of the war against Germany was in sight. On the Eastern Front, the Red Army was swallowing the Baltic States, surging across Poland and heading unstoppably towards the German capital. They traversed – and created – a hellish landscape. In July 1944, Soviet troops discovered Majdanek death camp, the first of the Nazi camps to be liberated. Its horrors were widely publicized – although the Soviet NKVD secret police repurposed Majdanek to imprison Polish nationalists.

Red Army troops committed many atrocities during their advance. In late October 1944, during the first Soviet incursion into East Prussia, villagers were murdered, and women raped and killed. The full-scale invasion of the same region in January 1945 embraced a systematic campaign of rape, murder and pillage. For ordinary Germans, a long-threatened nightmare was coming true. Across the Oder, Berlin lay barely 50 miles away from the Red Army.

Downfall

At 11.02 a.m. on 9 August 1945, a nuclear bomb nicknamed 'Fat Man' fell several thousand feet through a gap in thick clouds above the Japanese city of Nagasaki. When it was a little more than 1,500 feet from the ground, the plutonium core of the device exploded in a nuclear fission chain reaction, releasing energy equivalent to 21,000 tons of TNT. The explosion, including the massive 'mushroom' cloud pictured here, was spectacular. The destruction wrought on Nagasaki was even more so: around 40 per cent of the buildings were destroyed. Perhaps 40,000 people – almost all of them civilians – were killed instantly, and within six months, roughly the same number would succumb to the effects of exposure to massive doses of radiation.

'Fat Man' was the third nuclear device ever to be detonated. The first, in New Mexico on 16 July 1945, was the so-called Trinity Test, which demonstrated the success of the Manhattan Project – the American nuclear arms program. It confirmed US victory in the nuclear arms race with Germany and the USSR; it also made the deployment of a US atomic bomb overwhelmingly likely in the Far East, where Japanese defiance created intolerably high numbers of projected casualties for any invasion of mainland Japan. President Harry S. Truman – who succeeded to office on Roosevelt's death in April 1945 – was all too glad to sanction the use of a weapon that could obliterate Japanese cities with minimal danger to American lives, while sending a message to the USSR about America's potential post-war military supremacy. On 6 August, atomic warfare began with a uranium 'gun-type' bomb nicknamed 'Little Boy', which vaporized much of the Japanese city of Hiroshima. In the days after Nagasaki's destruction, US aircraft littered Japan with leaflets warning of their intention to repeat the atomic blasts until Emperor Hirohito surrendered his country.

The emperor finally did so on 14 August. When Hirohito's words were broadcast, it was the first address he had ever given to his people, albeit in a classical, courtly Japanese that was unintelligible to most of them. 'Should we continue to fight,' he said, 'not only would it result in an ultimate collapse and obliteration of the Japanese nation, but also it would lead to the total extinction of human civilization.' He was not very far from the truth.

Even without the atomic bombs, the death-throes of the Second World War were as terrible as anything that had preceded them. When 1945 dawned, Allied troops advancing on Germany from the west and their Soviet counterparts arriving from the east saw at first hand the sickening reality of the Nazi death camps. Yet as the camps fell, SS officers sent prisoners on 'death marches' to the Reich's interior, during which thousands more perished. The survivors were herded into other, overcrowded and disease-riddled camps, behind the lines.

Nevertheless, the lines themselves were disappearing. Between 16 April and 2 May, Soviet forces overran and destroyed Berlin, with massive loss of life on both sides and numerous crimes against civilians. Finally accepting that the end had arrived, Adolf Hitler committed suicide in his bunker on 30 April, an example followed by other leading Nazis in the days and weeks to follow, though some were captured and tried for war crimes. In Italy, Benito Mussolini was beaten and shot to death by partisans in late April. In Japan, the prime minister and general, Hideki Tojo, was eventually hanged for war crimes in 1948, and Emperor Hirohito's status was downgraded to constitutional monarch, a role he continued to play until his death in 1989.

Given everything that the Second World War had delivered, the announcement of VJ (Victory over Japan) Day, on 15 August 1945, was as much a cause for awful contemplation as it was for celebration. The war had killed between 70 million and 85 million people – roughly 3 per cent of the world's population. Like the First World War, the Second had harnessed all the greatest technological advances of its time and turned them to vicious and diabolical ends. The world would take decades to recover, and the only consolation was that for a time – to the present day, at least – people would recall its horrors and say to one another: never again.

Liberating the Camps

As the Allies captured Nazi-occupied territory, they saw at close hand the concentration and death camps. In late January 1945 the Red Army arrived at Auschwitz-Birkenau, to find around 6,000 prisoners in a dreadful condition. In the west, US troops arrived at Buchenwald on 11 April. There, over 20,000 prisoners remained, although an epidemic of typhus had killed many more. Four days later, General George Patton, commander of the Third Army, demanded that civilians from nearby Weimar be brought to Buchenwald to witness the bodies stacked naked in heaps and human beings reduced to skeletons.

The photographer Margaret Bourke-White arrived at Buchenwald on 15 April. She took this famous photograph that day and noted that although she used a flash, not one of the traumatized prisoners before her flinched or reacted to the light. Her camera lens provided a psychological barrier to the horrors of the camp. 'I hardly knew what I had taken until I saw prints of my own photographs,' she said.

Iwo Jima

The volcanic island of Iwo Jima ('Sulphur Island') lies roughly 650 miles (1000km) from Tokyo, halfway between Japan and the Mariana Islands. An airbase on Iwo Jima had allowed the Japanese air force to disrupt long-range US bombing raids from Saipan, so in February 1945 US Marines arrived to conquer it. They faced one of their most challenging and costly battles, particularly around the extinct volcano Mount Suribachi.

The Marines' assault began on 23 February, and although they took heavy casualties, they secured Mount Suribachi the same day. This is one of several images captured by Staff Sergeant Louis R. Lowery, who took photographs for the Marine Corps' *Leatherneck* magazine. The Marines shown are switching the first US flag that had been planted on the mountain for another, larger one, which could be seen from further away. A similar image of the same event (taken by Associated Press photographer Joe Rosenthal) became famous across the world, being used to sell US war bonds and even featuring on a postage stamp in 1945. Despite this triumphant scene, it took another month – and 23,000 US Marine casualties – to win Iwo Jima.

Dresden

On the night of 13 February 1945, more than 700 RAF Lancaster bombers arrived over the city of Dresden. RAF Bomber Command's justification for the attack was the city's use as a wartime transportation hub. But the massive firestorms that ensued, in which temperatures reached 1,000°C, destroyed more than military targets.

This photograph was taken from the viewing platform of the Rathausturm – the tower of the City Hall: it shows the wreckage caused by the firebombing, which burned out some 1,600 acres of the city and killed between 20,000 and 25,000 people. The statue in the foreground of this photograph, offering up this vista of abject ruination, is known as *Güte*, or Goodness.

Queasiness over Dresden's incineration began with Churchill, who in March 1945 said that 'the destruction of Dresden remains a serious query against the conduct of the Allied bombing'. The American writer Kurt Vonnegut, who was trapped there as a prisoner of war, called the experience 'carnage unfathomable'.

Crossing the Rhine

As US Marines fought on Iwo Jima, the American armies in Europe were arriving at the banks of the Rhine. Crossing this great western German river would also be symbolically powerful; even at the end of the First World War in 1918 the Allies had not made significant incursions on its eastern banks.

The Rhine was heavily defended. Although a US tank patrol seized Ludendorff Bridge at Remagen, most other permanent crossings were blown up on Hitler's orders. The Allies were therefore forced to use improvised pontoon bridges or landing craft. This photograph was taken aboard one of the latter: it shows troops of the US 89th Infantry Division crossing the Rhine near St Goar. The US Signal Corps photographer who took the picture recalled his bad luck at being assigned to a landing craft. 'We all tried to crawl under each other because the lead was flying around like hail,' he noted.

Despite stiff resistance, by 24 March the river was so secure that General Patton could stop while driving over one pontoon bridge to 'take a piss in the Rhine'. Ahead of him, Nazi resistance was petering out.

The Battle of Berlin

In spring 1945, Berlin, lying in eastern Germany, was closer to the Red Army than the Allied armies approaching from the Rhine. Knowing that the Allied Supreme Commander, Eisenhower, was ambivalent about forcing a march to reach the German capital first, Stalin whipped his own generals to make all haste to take it. The 'race to Berlin' brought more than 1.5 million Soviet troops to the outskirts of the city on 16 April. Their arrival began one of the most ferocious battles of the Second World War, in which the Red Army suffered some 350,000 casualties as they battered the Nazis' last ring of defences.

After a confused and desperate fight, in which many regular German units flocked west to surrender to the Americans or British rather than the Soviets, it took just two weeks for Berlin to fall. On 2 May, Red Army soldiers were in control of the Reichstag, mounting the roof and flying the Soviet flag with glee. On that day the Nazi garrison had given up, as General Helmuth Weidling signed the instrument of surrender.

The Führerbunker

'It is all lost, hopelessly lost,' Hitler said on 22 April, as news reached him that the Red Army had broken Berlin's defences. Two days previously, the Führer had celebrated his fifty-sixth birthday in this bunker within the besieged capital. For months he had been in denial about the German war effort and the implosion of the Nazi regime, insulated as he was from reality by layers of security and a long-standing addiction to powerful drugs.

Now, though, truth dawned. The war was lost. On 29 April Hitler married his girlfriend, Eva Braun; the next day he poisoned his dog, Blondi, then Braun took cyanide and Hitler shot himself. Josef and Magda Goebbels, also in the bunker, murdered their six children and killed themselves. Hitler left a will and testament true to his bigotry and delusion: he blamed Jews for the war and demanded a struggle to continue Nazism. He left behind a legacy of pointless hatred, genocide and destruction – and this pitiful room, photographed after it was pillaged on 1 May 1945.

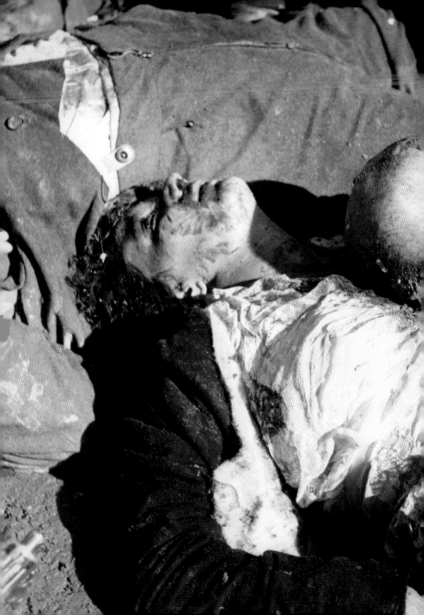

Mussolini's Death

Two days before Hitler committed suicide, on 28 April, his erstwhile fellow dictator Benito Mussolini was captured by Italian partisans and shot dead, along with his girlfriend Clara Petacci. They died near the village of Dongo, not far from Lake Como, but their corpses – photographed here – were brought to Milan on 29 April, where they were abused by crowds before being hung upside down outside a petrol station.

Mussolini's capture and death were preceded by the collapse of the Italian Social Republic – the Nazi puppet state over which he had nominally ruled since late 1943. This rump Fascist regime had been under pressure from its first moments, riven by factionalism and under attack from both the Allies and armed insurgents. By the end, Mussolini had been able to offer its citizens nothing but empty promises and bravado.

Milan fell to partisans on 25 April; within the week Il Duce's broken body was dangling there on public display and the SS commander in Italy, Karl Wolff, had negotiated surrender with the Allies.

Surrender

Hitler had named Admiral Karl Dönitz as his successor (not as Führer but as Reich President); but as Dönitz ruled from Flensburg, in northern Germany, the process of halting the war in Europe and dismantling the Nazi state began. This photograph shows the naval chief Admiral Hans-Georg von Friedeburg (*centre*), on the evening of 4 May, surrendering all forces in north-west Germany, the Netherlands and Denmark to the British commander in that sector, Field Marshal Montgomery (*seated, right*). The scene was witnessed by reporters and photographers, including a newsreel film crew from Pathé.

It was not the last such document to be signed. After several days of tense negotiation, a fuller instrument of unconditional military surrender – satisfactory to the Allied Supreme Commander, Eisenhower, as well as to the Soviet high command, represented by Marshal Zhukov – was formalized on the night of 8/9 May in Berlin. During the following weeks, the Flensburg government was rounded up and arrested. Admiral Friedeburg took a cyanide capsule and died on 23 May, avoiding the certain fate of being tried for war crimes.

The United Nations

US President Franklin D. Roosevelt died on 12 April, before he could witness the final collapse of the Axis forces he had devoted his last years to defeating. But among his many great legacies was the name he coined for the organization founded in 1945 to police the world and prevent future global wars. The United Nations (UN) was voted into existence at an international conference in San Francisco held between April and June; it was officially constituted on 24 October.

This photograph was taken at a sub-committee meeting of the San Francisco conference by Gjon Mili, the Albanian-born photographer who also pioneered freeze-frame 'stop-motion' photography. The face illuminated on the far left, smoking a pipe, belongs to Edward, Lord Halifax, the British Ambassador to Washington. The figure smoking a cigar is John Foster Dulles (*second right*), a career diplomat from a family of high-flying US public servants and a future Secretary of State. Dulles had promoted American membership of the UN's ill-fated predecessor, the League of Nations, and was keenly involved in drafting the terms on which the new organization was built.

Okinawa

With Germany and Italy beaten, Japan remained the only Axis power left to be defeated. Yet the scale of that task was dauntingly bloody, as proven by the battle for the Pacific island of Okinawa, whose airstrip was considered critical to the proposed invasion of Japan proper, pencilled for late 1945.

The joint US Army–Marines task force (with British naval support) sent to Okinawa staged the largest amphibious assault of the whole Pacific war, involving around 200,000 combat troops. More than 14,000 of them died in a battle that lasted from 1 April to 21 June and was nicknamed the 'typhoon of steel'.

The nonchalance evinced by these Marines is understandable. As Japanese defenders dug into the hillsides, the death toll rose. Around 100,000 Okinawan civilians were killed or committed suicide, and around the same number of Japanese military personnel also died. Nearly every building on Okinawa was destroyed and the tropical landscape ravaged. The result was an Allied victory but at appalling cost to both sides. Conservative estimates suggested that an invasion of mainland Japan might cost 200,000 American lives. It was a sobering thought.

Potsdam

The solution to the Japanese question was already forming in the mind of new US President Harry S. Truman (*seated, centre*) when he attended a conference in the Berlin suburb of Potsdam, which convened between 17 July and 2 August 1945. Truman hinted to Stalin (*seated, right*) that the USA had 'a weapon of unusual destructive force' that might do the job on its own. One way or another, the end was in sight.

So was the future. There were other new faces at Potsdam, as this photograph shows. A British general election had ousted Winston Churchill from office and replaced him by Clement Attlee (*seated, left*). Behind them stand (*left to right*) US Admiral William Daniel Leahy, the new British Foreign Secretary Ernest Bevin and US Secretary of State James Byrnes. These new men had pressing matters to discuss. Carving up and occupying defeated Germany, agreeing war reparations, drawing new borders for Poland and restraining Stalin's ambitions for communism in eastern Europe were all on the table. The second half of the twentieth century was coming rapidly into focus.

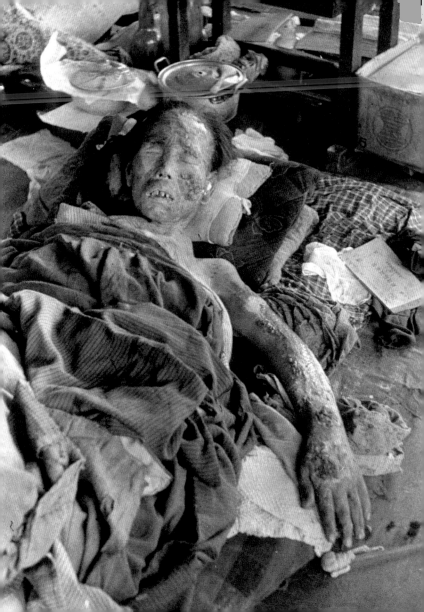

Hiroshima and Nagasaki

A USAAF B-29 Superfortress bomber named *Enola Gay*, after the pilot's mother, dropped the 'Little Boy' nuclear bomb over Hiroshima at 8.15 a.m. on 6 August 1945. When it exploded, in the words of one eyewitness, 'Hiroshima just didn't exist'. Temperatures reached around 3,000°C in the blast zone, and between 70,000 and 80,000 people died.

Yet this was not enough to coerce the Japanese high command into surrender. On 8 August the USSR finally declared war on Japan and sent 1.6 million troops into occupied Manchuria. Then, on 9 August, the 'Fat Man' nuclear device was detonated over Nagasaki. Once more, tens of thousands of people were killed instantly, and the same number again suffered fatal radiation poisoning. This photograph shows just one of the victims of the blast: a child suffering from terrible burns, clinging to life at an improvised hospital in a Nagasaki elementary school.

Despite the horrors of the blasts, and the threat of further attacks, it took until 14 August for Emperor Hirohito to announce the Japanese surrender.

VJ Day

Owing to the difference in time zones, it was evening on 14 August when news broke in the United States that Japan had quit the war. Formal surrender terms would not be signed until 2 September, but joy immediately swept the country.

This photograph shows the Brazilian performer Carmen Miranda dancing on a convertible car in the streets of Los Angeles. She gave an impromptu performance across the street from Grauman's Chinese Theater, at the intersection of Hollywood Boulevard and Orange Drive. (Today, a square there is named in her honour.) Of course, Victory over Japan (VJ) Day was not only celebrated in the USA. In Britain, Prime Minister Attlee announced a three-day public holiday.

In Tokyo, however, humiliation and misery reigned. Japan's capital had been wrecked by Allied firebombing raids in March. Now there was nothing for the dejected citizens to do but stand in the streets outside the Imperial Palace and weep.

The Nuremberg Trials

In 1943, Churchill, Roosevelt and Stalin had signed a joint declaration condemning the 'atrocities, massacres and cold-blooded mass executions which are being perpetrated by Hitlerite forces'. The Allies vowed to pursue the perpetrators 'to the uttermost ends of the earth' after the war. This promise motivated the International Military Tribunal, which opened in Nuremberg on 19 November 1945.

Charges of war crimes and crimes against humanity were drawn up against twenty-four leading Nazis. The men in the front row here include (*from left*) Hermann Göring, Joachim von Ribbentrop and Wilhelm Keitel. In the back row can be seen (*far left*) Admiral Karl Dönitz, (*fifth and sixth from left*) General Alfred Jodl, Franz von Papen and (*eighth from left*) Albert Speer, Hitler's friend, architect and minister for armaments. Twelve of the accused were sentenced to death by hanging, including Göring, Jodl, Keitel and von Ribbentrop. Others, such as Dönitz and Speer, were given long prison sentences. But many prominent Nazis escaped the noose. Justice was served – but not completely.

Escaping Justice

Hermann Göring was found guilty of all charges at Nuremberg. The judges called him 'the moving force, second only to [Hitler]'. On 15 October 1946, the night before his execution day, he obtained a cyanide capsule and killed himself in his cell. This photograph shows his corpse before it was burned and his ashes thrown in the Isar River. Many other Nazis also cheated justice. Hitler shot himself. Josef Goebbels committed suicide. Heinrich Himmler took cyanide while in British custody. Heinrich Müller, chief of the Gestapo, disappeared and was never found. Dr Josef Mengele, who performed cruel human 'experiments' at Auschwitz, fled to Brazil and died in 1979. Perhaps the most famous case of a Nazi evading justice was that of Adolf Eichmann, a senior SS officer who played a leading role in organizing the Final Solution. Eichmann escaped a US detention camp in 1945, fled to Argentina and was only captured by Israeli intelligence agents in 1960. He was hanged after a trial in Jerusalem in 1962. 'To sum it all up,' he reflected in an interview, 'I must say that I regret nothing.'

Index of Events and Themes